timothy morton / dominic boyer
their relations & companions

hyposubjects

on becoming human

CCC2 Irreversibility

Series Editors: Tom Cohen and Claire Colebrook

The second phase of 'the Anthropocene,' takes hold as tipping points speculated over in 'Anthropocene 1.0' click into place to retire the speculative bubble of "Anthropocene Talk". Temporalities are dispersed, the memes of 'globalization' revoked. A broad drift into a de facto era of managed extinction events dawns. With this acceleration from the speculative into the material orders, a factor without a means of expression emerges: climate panic.

timothy morton / dominic boyer
their relations & companions

hyposubjects

on becoming human

( )

OPEN HUMANITIES PRESS

London 2021

First edition published by Open Humanities Press 2021

Print ISBN 978-1-78542-096-2
PDF ISBN 978-1-78542-095-5
eBook ISBN 978-1-78542-097-9

OPEN HUMANITIES PRESS

Open Humanities Press is an international, scholar-led open access publishing collective whose mission is to make leading works of contemporary critical thought freely available worldwide. More at http://openhumanitiespress.org

Contents

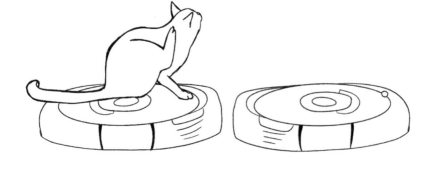

For Jade Hagan, Brijzha, Claire, Olivia, Simon, Black Lives Matter,
Extinction Rebellion Youth and Generation Z

Reporter: What do you think of Western Civilization?
Gandhi: I think it would be a good idea.

The women's movement is not only international.
It is planetary. *Carla Lonzi*

Don't grow up. Grow down. *Chris Robertson*

0.00001: a socially distanced preface

Stuff is happening. The book *Hyperobjects* is now in a way irrele-vant—everyone knows, everyone intuitively *feels* (which is much more important) what a hyperobject is. Coronavirus is everywhere. You can't see it. It operates on all kinds of different scales—terrify-ing interpersonally or if you're being forced back to work or school; weirdly amazing at demonstrating a world with less or no neoliberal churning, and fomenting planet-scale collective awareness and action.

It's pure poetry that right after we all started going into "lockdown" around Earth—really a kind of opening up to a less frantic and more caring way of being—Black Lives Matter exploded around Earth too. We've always thought the struggle against racism was fundamental to opening up a genuinely *future future* in which different things might be possible. Things other than the algorithmic churning of capital-ism, which don't let's forget is enabled by the slavery that is primitive accumulation. That so many non-Black people, around Earth, sud-denly realized how cheap and violent life is in the USA (we know, we live in the South), and mobilized to care radically for that life, and in particular, the Black lives that matter—it's nothing short of a stun-ning promise of a new architecture, liquid, in motion, consisting of crowds of people tearing up the slower, more oppressive architecture of shops and statues.

It's a moment at which you can feel overlapping structures of feel-ing, to borrow Raymond Williams's suggestive but never very well theorized term. In a way, structure of feeling is to ideology as visu-alization is to an image. The former is evanescent, "flimsy" even, it could collapse at any moment, you haven't written it down yet—and that's why it's good. That's why it's a kind of mist from the future. This future mist eats away at the statues of the past better than the strongest acid. There is a feel, not just a feeling, of planet-scale aware-ness. Of belonging that isn't fascist. Social distancing should be called social intimacy. My decision to avoid you and wear a mask means I want you to live. My inability to see the workers in the supermarket because I'm in quarantine is an uncanny way of imagining them, like "don't think of a pink elephant," and joining them. A mask says "I have mercy on you."

The chaotic and violent non-response of the USA to the cri-sis has some salutary effects. You can see, by looking at the graph of our stupidity, how the virus hasn't gone anywhere. Some neoliberal economies just avoided it for a while. And white men (trust us, together we've been to about twelve airports since March) are the ones who think they don't need or shouldn't wear a mask, that a mask is a gag, not mercy-wear. That tells you everything you need to know about their idea of what a "subject" is (a master) and what an "object" is (a slave).

And it also tells you, in the moment of Black Lives Matter, that their time is most definitely up. So death to these hypersubjects, as we call them in this far-from-tome—we/you don't get to destroy Earth any more at the expense of everyone else. Yeah we know, we are white guys. We know.

0.0001: think small

Check the warning label before you read any further. It might go something like: what follows is an exercise in flimsy and chaotic thinking. You are bound to be disappointed. No, seriously. Don't get your hopes up. Especially if you are looking for something like a "theory of the hyposubject." Good luck finding it in this heap. A lot of what is happening here frankly doesn't make very much sense. Yes, we know we ought to be ashamed of ourselves. But it all comes from a sincere spirit of trying to help. Which, for beings like us, means becoming less. Sometimes it takes two to unmake one. Our I is hallucinatory, a we that affirms and argues with itself by turns. It began as a series of salad- and kombucha-fueled dialogues in 2014 that have been subsequently compressed, sliced into pieces, remixed, augmented, and further fermented in the sun and shade. 2014 was a few years before it became obvious that fascism had returned full-force to the world alongside (thankfully) socialism. Liberalism is still the same: ever the smug zombie that thinks it's owed eternity.

We wrote a few years before "climate change" became "climate emergency." Premonitions and underestimations abound in what follows. But we believe our original intuition still holds. The time of hypersubjects is ending. Their desert-apocalypse-fire-and-death cults aren't going to save them this time. Meanwhile the time of hyposubjects is beginning. And they will provide their own theories, thank you very much. If you know all that already, then maybe don't waste your time with this. We're happy to just be bystanders as hyposubjects come into their own and world themselves. But we also hope to lend a hand as needed. One person's junkyard is another person's playground. The weird little hall of mirrors we've created here is filled with nightmares and jokes and distractions and shards of utopias. We're keen to share this haunt with anyone intrigued by it. Basically anyone who feels the madness that accompanies a world turning itself inside out. If you're still here, welcome. We begin (again) by ending.

What do we think of human beings? We think they would be a very good idea.

We live in a time of hyperobjects, of objects too massive and multiphasic in their distribution in time and space for humans to fully comprehend or experience them in a unitary way. A black hole is a kind of hyperobject, a biosphere is another. But many of the hyperobjects that concern us have human origins. For example, global warming. Or antibiotics. Or plastic bags. Or capitalism. These hyperobjects exceed and envelop us like a viscous fog, they make awkward and unexpected appearances, they inspire hypocrisy and lameness and dread.

A certain kind of human has helped usher the world into the hyperobjective era. Let's call them hypersubjects. You will recognize them as the type of subjects you are invited to vote for in elections, the experts who tell you how things are, the people shooting in your schools, the mansplainers from your Twitter feed. Hypersubjects are typically but not exclusively white, male, northern, well-nourished, modern in all senses of the term. They wield reason and technology, whether cynically or sincerely, as instruments for getting things done. They command and control, they seek transcendence, they get very high on their own supply of dominion. Do you want to know what is increasingly irritating hypersubjects? That hyperobjects are whispering in their ears that this being and time they have fashioned in their own image and for their own convenience is dying. The voices in their heads say that there is no time for hypersubjects any more. It is hyposubjectivity rather than hypersubjectivity that will become the companion of the hyperobjective era.

So, as hypersubjects seeking to reform, we have begun in a Roomba-like way to consider the political potentiality of hyposubjects. Although hyposubjectivity sounds a bit like an abject condition of being forced to endure and suffer the effects of viscous forces like climate change and capital, we wonder whether that sense of weakness and insignificance and lack of knowledge and agency is actually what needs embracing. Looking backwards, the road to our present condition is paved with mastery of things, people and creatures and with weird faith in our species' alleged ability to always know more and better. This project may end up resembling a book but we hope you will experience it as a game, maybe a role playing game because we all like costumes and because this is a game that needs more players. It is open source and open access for collective reflection and elaboration. For the moment, here are some things we've been thinking:

∞ Hyposubjects are the native species of the Anthropocene and only just now beginning to discover what they may be and become.

∞ Like their hyperobjective environment, hyposubjects are also multiphasic and plural, not-yet, neither here nor there, less than the sum of their parts. They are in other words subscendent rather than transcendent. They do not pursue or pretend to absolute knowledge and language let alone power. Instead they play, they care, they adapt, they hurt, they laugh.

∞ Hyposubjects are necessarily feminist, antiracist, colorful, queer, ecological, transhuman and intrahuman. They do not recognize the rule of androleukoheteropetromodernity and the apex species behavior it epitomizes and reinforces. But they also hold the bliss-horror of extinction fantasies at bay because hyposubjects' befores, nows and afters are many.

∞ Hyposubjects are squatters and bricoleuses. They inhabit the cracks and hollows. They turn things inside out and work with scraps and remains. They unplug from carbon gridlife and hack and redistribute its stored energies for their own purposes.

∞ Hyposubjects make revolutions where technomodern radar can't glimpse them. They patiently ignore expert advice that they don't or can't exist. They are skeptical of efforts to summarize them, including everything we have just said.

In sum, for the moment, the transcendent hypersubject continues to stalk the earth. But he is doing so in an increasingly flickering, even spectral way; his monophasic being is perpetually out of sync. Half-aware that his time is past, he lashes out violently, pouts, negates any alternative, bargains for salvational machines and afterlife redemptions. You might pity him had he not left so much ruin and despair in his wake. As we write, huge numbers of these distressed creatures are climbing inside of balloons called Donald Trump, Boris Johnson, Jair Bolsonaro, inflating them, hoping to fly away. But as in Alfonso Cuarón's film Gravity, what awaits us instead is fabricating a future out of ruins and preparing for a long perilous voyage back to earth. That future will belong to hyposubjects; if we wish to thrive we will become human again as hyposubjects.

I hyperobjects, narcissism, white boys, looping, teenagers, toys, games, squats, gut bacteria

Here we go. Let me get this folder open. Ready? 1, 2, 3. Check, check, check.

Check, check. Here we go… So what I wanted to suggest is that this all has to begin with hyperobjects. And then the story moves to hyposubjects. But, first things first, we need to hear about hyperobjects. Right. Well, I was thinking the same thing. When I first was told the word "hyposubject"—by two people, one of whom was you—I thought I'm not about subjects at all. You know? But then I started thinking, well, this isn't really about my prejudices about subjects, is it? It's actually about the stance that us lot, assuming that we're humans, have in light of what's been going on. And it's about why can't Hegel-inspired Marxists and OOO Marxists get along? And in general, how come scholars can't model refraining from the narcissistic chewing-off of limbs that afflicts the left? It's true. White boys fencing over concepts is just about the worst thing in the little village of academic life.

It's about white boys getting with the program and cutting themselves down to size. The climate emergency has at least one ironically progressive facet. White boys now get to feel what it's like to be just about everyone else, everyone else having suffered from white boys since boys and wheat began to relate symbiotically. If you farm that stuff in northern Europe, you need to turn into a more efficient solar panel to get the vitamin D. Whiteness is all about what elsewhere I've called agrilogistics, and agrilogistics is the first wave of the catastrophe we call the Anthropocene.

It's about older white boys trying to help out younger beings. I recently interviewed Extinction Rebellion Youth. My only question to them was, "How can I be of assistance to you?" Without looking like a mansplain-y uncle or a narcissistic grabber of bullhorns. I don't mind if you think I look like that, dear reader. I would just like to try my best to not make this be all about me. Or me either. Well, it's going to be hard for anyone to find an unadulterated me in here.

Can you imagine what it's like being in Generation Z? As much as I dislike PR advertising labels, I'm fond now of being an X-er. X is a high scoring letter in Scrabble, for a kickoff. And the X implies something fun and foolish about one's parents, the Boomers: "Who on earth are these people? Oh—they're our children!" We understand a little bit what it's like, in an existential inner sort of a way at least. But Generation Z rightly cries out that everyone else did it to them—fucked up planet Earth, and now it's on them to fix it? Jesus H Christ. Everyone else, for twelve and a half thousand years. Marx talks about history weighing like a nightmare on the brains of the living. He had no freakin clue.

In a way, how dare we try to help, given that we don't even understand fully the problem we've created for them, and given how we love to shock everyone and make them feel stupid and evil, shocking them with climate and extinction data dumps on page one of the newspaper, and paralyzing them with eco guilt on the editorial page? But then again, who else is going to do it? It's like that sentiment of Beckett that Adorno loved—I can't go on, I must go on...fail better. Fail better and fail often.

And I think that what's been going on roughly for the last two hundred years has been realizing that we are surrounded and permeated by a large number of extremely big things, relative to us. These things are massively distributed in time and space, such that it's very hard to even see that they are entities at all. And I'm thinking of things like global warming mostly, and pollution—you know, that old word from the 1970's—and radiation. But also, really you could apply this to anything—big things that are difficult to think—including, actually, the notion of human. Maybe that's a good place to start. Because paradoxically, I think that realizing that you are human is really only possible in light of these hyperobjects. Sure.

In other words, I now know that I'm made of nonhumans, and that that entails evolution. And I also know that when I turn the ignition in my car, that's a statistically meaningless action. I don't mean to harm anything when I do that. And yet at the same time, scaled up to earth magnitude—and now we're talking about billions of key turnings every few minutes, ongoing for several decades—I am contributing to global warming. And not little me. But me, as a member of this thing called human, which is not an abstract concept anymore, you know, as with many of our beloved philosophers, but actually as a physical entity. And, of course, as a force.

Yes, at the same time, which is very hard to point to. I can't point to discrete instances of it. Nevertheless, it's happening. And so, somehow, for good or bad, there's a dominant, more real segment of things like me, that now gets modulated.

It's sort of like essentialism—there is this thing called species... (salad and disco music). And so, these things are very unthinkable, and yet necessary to think. As the human species, we are a hyperobject insofar as we are this gigantic thing distributed across space-time.

That's confusing in a number of different ways. It's logically confusing, and it's category-bending, and it's real and it's there, but it's not your grandfather's idea of real and there. And that's kind of it, really. That's hyperobjects.

What got me thinking about the hyposubject was the extent to which that hyperobjective condition, which I think is a very good diagnosis, implicates life in the Anthropocene. It's more than that, too—but just to stay within the context of the Anthropocene and global warming for a moment—that it creates a paradoxical situation. On the one hand, we're massive, and have this activity that is global in scale and geological, perhaps. And at the same time, we're also smaller than we've ever been, less than we've ever been, too. For me the hyperobjective condition also summons the hyposubjective as its companion. I mean, we exist as both at the same time.

A hyposubject is how a hyperobject feels about itself.

Indeed, partly. The other side of it is that we still have to cope with the fact that we have this sort of massive, narcissistic attachment to our own sense of distinctiveness as a species, and this sense that we're at the top of a great chain of being, and that we are the ones who may have gotten ourselves into the Anthropocene but we're also the saviors, the only ones who are going to get us out of this situation. Those attachments are hyperobjective as well. That mass overestimation of what humanity, capital H, can achieve. Yes.

Reader, can you see a funny thing about this book already? We decided not to present it in dialogue form, and not to use the first person plural, so that it comes off like one of those wonderful paragraphs of my favorite modernist, Virginia Woolf, where there are about three or four people, and not just humans but some kind of assemblage of humans, birds and snails for example, all joined together in the stream of consciousness, bursting out of the skin-encapsulated ego, a sort of dam burst or leak of narcissistic energy ... as Jacques Derrida observed, there is no one narcissism, and there is not narcissism versus non-narcissism. Imagine how narcissistic it would be to claim that one didn't have it! And then imagine not eating, because narcissism is why you eat, why you let things inside. And eco-politics is all about the beings you let inside. Symbiosis is just that. Think of a single celled organism floating through the ocean. Gulp! "Shit! Did I just swallow poison?" they think. That's the phenomenology of symbiosis—an uneasy relationship with others, with the neighbor, uneasiness as a basis for benevolence, in fact. Try to delete the unease and you get planet death if you wash rinse repeat.

So Derrida argues that there are in fact many different narcissisms that are more or less extended, and the eco-political idea would be to try to extend one's narcissism to include as many humans and as many nonhumans as possible.

Then we made up this rule, that every five years two other people must volunteer to write this book all over again. Well, at least two other people, maybe it could be one hundred. And of course we're not in a position to call forth any volunteers. We hope that this means the book becomes a sort of videogame that helps to boot up this new kind of subject, the hyposubject. Or you might think of it as the ancient weathered toy left by a forgotten child in the sandbox of the park where all the neighborhood kids play. It's missing a leg or a wheel and somehow its abject incompleteness is what draws the next player in.

This is what I like so much about *Attack on Titan*, the image in particular of the small hunted hyposubject looking out at the massive predatory hypersubject self. That image captures the subjective condition of the contemporary. Part of you thinks, hyposubject, and conjures a kind of abject image. But part of the question here is whether we can also discern for the hyposubject a non-abject condition? Is there a way of being hyposubjective that can actually help to defeat hypersubjectivity? Like when one of the protagonists of *Attack on Titan* learns how phase-shift into titan form to help defend his friends from being devoured by the other titans.

It's time. There's a kind of simmering paralysis where we are right now. Yes. And you know, one neat thing that you just did is to confuse, a little bit, subject and object, which are the perennial boxes that we put things in. But I would also like do a shout out here to narcissism. Do it. I'd like to slightly modify that sentence. I'd like to say that wounded narcissism thinks of itself as the top of the food chain. In other words, once you've figured out—semi-consciously, after several thousand years of an agricultural project that was doomed within a few hundred years of its beginning, that then went viral for no good reason, like neoliberalism—once you know that it's objectively failing, then you have a narcissistic wound.

The old Greek for that would be hamartia, some kind of inner wound or flaw. And the appropriate mode, then, you think for working this all through is tragedy. You know, I'm at the top of the food chain, but it's lonely at the top. It's tough at the top. To me, that's wounded narcissism. In other words, one of the ways that we get towards hyposubjectively accommodating ourselves to hyperobjects—or just living the hyperobject—is through some kind of rapprochement precisely with narcissism, with the "narcissistic self-actualization" stuff that wrong, bad people did in the 1970s.

I'm sort of with Derrida here. If you destroy the narcissistic relation, you destroy in advance any possibility of relation to the other.

Because in a certain sense, narcissism is a feedback loop to "yourself." I mean, it isn't really you in the first place—there's probably a much better way of talking about it if you do yoga, which is that you know, you have these channels. And they're not really you. Now I've broken another rule, which is, you must never mention channels in polite scholarship. But somehow, we have to, maybe break some rules here to get where we need to be in thinking this through. And that brings me to thinking about abjection, actually. Which is yes, how to work through it. And the direction through for me, most honestly and least violently, would be underneath or within. Because one of the complaints about ecological politics is that the Nazis thought it up.

Of course, you know, the Nazis were all about abjection when they projected it onto classes of people that they strove to eliminate, just as one might strive to eliminate a class of pests that were interfering with your agricultural project, say around 10,000 BCE. But since that's impossible—once we scale it up to earth magnitude and geological time—it's impossible, quickly enough, to strip away all the stuff that's sticking to you. And in a way, it's ontologically impossible, because you're made of this other stuff. And so somehow, abjection is not something you can get rid of.

And so, the Nazi possibility looms in the background. Are we going to do something even more violent, to achieve a way to relate to these big-scale entities? Or is it possible to go through, underneath the abjection to a place which is more playful, maybe, or open, but sort of inside the abjection? Because I think you and I don't want to stay in tragedy mode forever. Not just because it sucks, but because it's a symptom of the problem that we've been in, that we find ourselves caught in the headlights of our own doings.

Absolutely. A couple of thoughts on looping. I take from Freud, the early Freud, a model of the psyche constituted on the basis of hallucinatory loops, the primary process archiving impressions of pleasure, satisfaction, relief, planting charges that then almost magnetically pull new experiences toward them. The psychic apparatus wants each new experience to fit somewhere within archive of pleasures past so we are at our psychic cores always hallucinating madly. And now we face the unenviable challenge of, while still hallucinating madly, also trying to disrupt our current pleasuring loops, because those loops now have produced catastrophic oscillations as scaled up to the planetary level. So I've become interested in the figure of the teenager, in resuscitating the teenager, as opposed to, say, the typical general salvational category of "youth."

What is specific socially and culturally about "the teenager" is that you have a biotically adult, reproductive subject, who is at the same time forced into a state of suspension, restrained from attaining adult social and political capacities. It's a state we typify as simmering conflict, but less often as suspended potentiality. In some way, it's an abject state.

But it's actually also a profoundly non-abject state, an epic state even. In the course of the reproductive cycle, each generation inherits an enormous revolutionary potential that summons in turns an enormous repressive apparatus whose long game is to force a cathexis with the dominant structures of the adult world. We have to earn our adult pleasures and powers, sacrificing transformative potential for reproductive capacity bit by bit, and I suppose you could even argue that that's fine as long as the looping mechanism isn't itself catastrophic. But now we're basically all teenagers, being fucked over by an adult world that is repressing our transformative powers but that only really has death to offer us in exchange. So what we need is a strategy for breaking the loop. We need an escape trajectory.

It's fun that we're using a PR marketing category ("teens") against the PR that maintains the current status quo.

So what we're talking about in a way is the Foucauldian care of the self. And, what we're also talking about is appropriating a category from within consumerism: the teenager. So, in other words, this is also working with abjection. We have always been consumerists. Now we really are consumerists. But even Neanderthals, as far as I'm concerned, would have loved Coca-Cola Zero. And so, rather than rejecting that category, or the dispositif that categorizes things in that way, we use it, as opposed to trying to find an escape route that wouldn't seem to be it but ends up being it by resisting in the classic way: 'I'm not a consumerist.' Exactly. Because the circuit of resistance belongs to the same loop. Right. And so how to find the escape hatch, which could conceivably also be inside it or underneath it. I just think that's dope.

Which brings me to thinking also about the ludic. Because that's also, to my mind, something we associate with teenagers, this explosive ludic quality. If we're also thinking about hyposubjective qualities that we need to maintain and to nurture then the ludic is one of them. This has to be the age of squatting and occupation of the hyperobjective terrain. It's not resistance in a typical literal, political way, like speaking truth to power. Not that there's anything wrong with it, but I doubt that speaking truth to power will be enough to disrupt our hyperobjective condition.

You've already said something here which is very deep. First of all, the hyposubject is how we live the hyperobject and then living the hyperobject is squatting in it. I actually think that to be a thing at all is to be playful, so it would be more accurate to live that way. And I also think that interdependence requires us to realize that we're all hypocrites, with incomplete toys at the political, philosophical, and psychic levels. Waiting to be spun together like EPs in a disco or something. But somehow, the attempt, including many environmentalist attempts so far, is so often really serious, and has tried to abolish play. And precisely wants to abolish consumerism because it's too much enjoyment, too much play, I think that's a big stumbling block. In my class yesterday, one of the students from your department, a guy named M——, who I think is terrific, came and did a great presentation on Bataille. He's a genius.

Specifically on the need for orgiastic recycling. I think this is what you're talking about, too. That the sober earnestness, and to be frank, the technocratic character of much of the resistance discourse and apparatus at our disposal, makes the future feel very forlorn. Even if it were to win, would you want to live in that world? Maybe it would be sustainable, but it would be, again, this bleak land of bare existence. And this is where I have to say that I'm still find myself troublingly enchanted by Marx, by the idea that one must pass through modernity and capitalism to get someplace better. Absolutely, I agree one hundred percent. The past was not great—just look around you, it's still here. There is no going back to the primitive condition. The primitivism itself is a kind of false romance. But rather the idea is to somehow survive through this process, to try to perhaps realize a world in which it's possible to have abundance and play and not destroy the planet and other life forms along the way.

Right. And also, given that—first of all, two things. Just on Marx, in particular, let's not forget that production doesn't mean what, say for example, Fordism or ergonomics thinks it means which is efficiency, in the name of just carrying on existing. Production is pleasure. Right? It's the evolution of the senses. It's you eating a peach. And in the bigger picture, since I am saying that all ideas and entities are toys, Marx—let's have him in there—the question is not, what's the real toy? The one toy to rule them all. The question is more, what kinds of toys are we going to fit to other toys? And this makes us a little bit Lyotardian, postmodernist in a way. But I even like that. I like the idea of realizing that I'm actually wearing these weird flared trousers from 1971. But now in a kind of ecological way rather than in an "oh everything is just a construct" kind of way. Which is itself a symptom of the very modernity that that kind of discourse is trying to exit. And so somehow we're taking the postmodernism, we're taking the Marxism, we're taking the environmentalism, and instead of deciding what's better than them, we're sort of putting them together into little toys that could maybe encourage people to make more toys.

And maybe toys are even better than rhizomes because toys are very unique and distinct somehow. There's not some intrinsic property of them that's good as opposed to non-toys. Everything is a toy so that there are no non-toys, and they're not good insofar as they are fluid or not, or capable of being collected or not, because that's still setting up some kind of "something's better than something else; something's more real than something else."

It's more practical, it's like, "let's make some toys for people to play with," and we're doing that right now, and "let's do that in the name of an intense performance, of incorporating as many other entities as possible." I'll say this to link this back to the previous point about production. We have a lot of toy making already that's very much wedded to a particular kind of Taylorist, Fordist industrial apparatus. That abundance of mass-marketed toys, and not just games of monopoly, but also all the epistemic toys that we have and like to live with.

For heaven's sake, let's not do a shout out to gameification, which reduces people to winners and losers of games, who are then fireable or payable insofar as they are no longer typing or meeting with people or coming up with ideas, but succeeding in playing the game. And that's what games contribute in that sense. A constant reinvestment in the way things are. The intolerable way things are. It's saying that this particular neoliberal model isn't a toy, it's the toy factory. You can play with all the toys you want, as long as you don't make the factory into a toy, and change that.

That's what we need to highlight here: turning the factory into a toy in its broadest sense. The industrial order that has contributed massively to the disruption of planetary ecology has to become toyed with. You can have a similar discussion about the need for experiments. But I actually like toys more as a concept because they don't obviously belong to the apparatus of modern laboratory science. It's a real problem for actual engineers, because they get paid by corporations. But in order to make things that the corporations want, they have to make a lot of toy things. And then the corporation decides this toy is not a toy, it's our product. That's the bit that sucks for the engineer, in the same way that the dismissal of the humanist as someone who just toys around without any reference to pacemakers at all, or to scientistic factoids that nobody believes in, is just superficially playing. So, on the one hand, we have making toys in a teleological way, in a way that will end up with something that isn't a toy. Or we have just making toys in a completely superficial way that leaves official reality completely unmessed with.

Haraway talks about play in a kindred way, play as the raw opportunism of emergence, play as a vital ally for critique since play commits itself to ways of being-in-the-world that are not fully functionalized.

Exactly. I like the term *prototype*, too, from the world of design or engineering as another alternative. But *prototype* has a certain heaviness to it. Especially if you think of it as a blueprint, a kind of formalized, rationalized planning instrument. Pointing in the direction of the real one. But prototypes can also be fun. They can be mischievous. They can be uncertain and incomplete. And in that way I think they're more toy-like. Which is why, dear listener, we are calling this "on becoming-human" (laughter).

Or maybe "un-becoming-human." We may have to put a further qualification in there. You see, because whatever this is, it is not even a prototype. Don't take this book as a model for how to be. No, no. It's not a blueprint. It's just a pair of twisted, intelligent people, playing with toys—and their salads—And their salads, and various other life forms. So in a certain way, this isn't a map. This project isn't a map. It's more like a bit of territory in which we've...

Squatted. About this much, about two square inches of it, that we're squatting. Squat the hyperobject. That's the new t-shirt that everybody has to wear. That t-shirt needs to be made. Is this the Introduction? Because if it is, I'm just noticing that we're doing it. It's not unpleasant. It's true. Something's happening.

I think we might both have the same surrealistic, associative program running. I think it has to be a surrealist project. I don't think this can be anything but a surrealist project. All the best people and projects are surrealist anyway. Yes. Which is why we're going to talk a lot about Iceland. We'll talk about Iceland. We'll talk about the Situationists. I'm sure other things will make an appearance as well. They will. They will, dear reader.

The hyposubjective condition is one with great generative potential. That much we certainly agree on. Yes. To recap: It can be experienced as an abject condition. There is that side of it. Being crushed. Being crushed. Being devoured. I think that is the critical discourse we have available, especially when we look at environmental and ecological literature. And honestly I'm very sympathetic to that language, because I understand the feeling that there's a kind of predatory apparatus that's consuming us. On the other hand, is that worldview adequate to help us to escape the predators? Or even to understand them better? If we can't escape them, at least to know what they are?

So somehow we have to go from feeling crushed—the honesty of feeling crushed—to realizing that actually we're not completely consumed. We're actually hanging on to the teeth of this hyperobject. We are in it. We are it, in terms of being human. And at the same time, the very fact that we can notice that, indicates that we're not. Indeed. And my Hegelian point about that would be: once you actually can name something like a hyperobject, it begins to lose its hold. Because knowledge only arrives at the end of something's concretization, not at the beginning, in your typical dialectical cycle of realization that is. So I think the fact that we can now identify hyperobjects and hyposubjects is itself a hopeful sign. Hyperobjects were much more efficacious when they were operating in the shadows. Before we could name them, before we could actually conceive of them, even in their barest outline, as objects is when they were most dangerous. The era we're living in is a fascinating, complex and hopeful one. Neoliberalism is crumbling, or its truth claims have been dispelled, to an extent. Yet, we don't have an –ism capable of replacing it, and that's a good thing. That means that we're in a sort of interim phase. This is the time of toys, the time of occupations, and the time of a certain playful kind of epistemic excess—before another power/knowledge episteme sucks us back in.

So let's use that. As you know, I've had my thoughts about Hegel. Let's hear a couple of thoughts. Let's bring all the different toymakers in. Basically we're not saying that because the subject, or Geist, comprehends the hyperobject, therefore, there is no hyperobject. We're not saying that the most real thing is the Geist, whatever that is, and that it uses some kind of blank screen, to foment its own self-knowing.

It's almost the inverse. It's like the more we know the hyperobjects, the more vivid they become by definition. It's just pure accumulation of data. And yet and at the same time, the more open and profound, and therefore playful, becomes our...what is that? We could call it subjectivity. We could call it Dasein. We could call it inner space. We've got all these words that don't really work anymore. So that there's actually a kind of asymmetry between the increasing perceived vividness and power of things like evolution and global warming and the felt sense of wiggle room. So that we're not going to say, "well because we're such clever shits and we've brought this to light, it doesn't have any hold." I mean precisely that it doesn't have a complete, total grip. That's absolutely the case.

It's more like what we're saying is, "this is for real" and "we can deal with it" at the same time. This isn't something that is just another way for us to be the most powerful being on earth. But it's actually a way for us to notice that we are weakly here, in the same way actually that our species is weak. Right now, extinction is quite clear.

And we're doing it. And so the notion of us being possibly extinct has become quite clear.

And so hyperobjects are finite—that's the other thing about them. They're not actually infinite, dark prisons. They're actually finite things that are toys, they're just really super super big. So you just have to think of a super super clever way of playing with them, as opposed to thinking "oh, they're the top level," or "they're demonic, intrinsically horrific things." I think this is your point, isn't it? The feeling of being caught in the headlights only goes that far. And then what happens then? If it's not about pretending that it's not happening?

It's about being able to reinhabit and remodulate the excessiveness that led to those hyperobjects in the first place, but to put it toward conditions that will, we hope, negate certain iterations of them. I mean, the hyperobjects likely are here to stay—I think that's part of what you're saying—and perhaps the hyposubjects, too. So it's not about pursuing negation ultimately but rather about remaking a relationship. I think the work of the hyposubject is precisely to find a better way of inhabiting a world of hyperobjects like the one that we live in. "Better" is obviously a loose term, but we know it when we feel it. And if that's not enough we have moral and ethical philosophy to lean on.

First of all, squatting is so much more interesting than dwelling. We have to squat. And also be mobile. It's also kind of an abject word for existing or inhabiting whatever. It's really pejorative. It's a word that people use about other people, even when they're referring to themselves. Being. Squatting. Thinking. The term came back to me in again talking about Jón and Jóga Gnarr who are humans we'll be talking about from time to time. Jón and other stiob performers have done this work of inhabiting caricatures of authoritative discourse, the language of power, language of the state, where you're never sure whether they're sincere or whether it's some ironic act. I described that in an essay as squatting within the authoritative discourse. Another part of the authoritative discourse we need to squat in is the discourse on climate change, climate science, global warming. This has to be a discourse that we can also inhabit in a playful way.

What events like Icelandic genius comedian Jón Gnarr's Best Party teach us is that it was play itself that reinvigorated politics. It was not about having a better argument or a greater number of facts on one's side. It was instead the willingness for someone to squat in the authoritative expert position and to play in it like an actor would that made people want to return to a political sphere that had been evacuated of purpose for so long.

One further association is how this works with the law. Because clearly squatting is something that seems to be illegal and yet is, we are claiming, a condition of any thing at all. You know there are bacteria squatting in my stomach. They don't even pay you rent.

They don't pay me rent. In many ways I'm paying them. And sometimes to my cost. And they're hyposubjects, too. The hyposubject is the bacteria in your gut. The hyposubject is Haraway's OncoMouse. It's not just about humans. I think we have to be very clear about that, too. The hyposubject is not a just human condition, although humans participate in that condition. True. I claim that the Anthropocene is the first truly anti-anthropocentric concept because it is borne out of realizing that you are a weak, fragile entity that could go extinct, that is made of other entities that aren't you, and that you coexist with these other entities and utterly relate with them.

This is another thing I wanted to say about the dilemma of working in an age of knowing this stuff about the planet. Because of interdependence, there's always at least one piece missing from the ethical political jigsaw that you make. In other words, in order to be nice to the bunny rabbits, I have to not be nice to the bunny rabbit parasites. There's always one entity that I'm leaving out of my ethical concerns, my political project, you see. There's always some excluded being, precisely because nothing is excludable from this circuit. And that's a weird kind of position to get in there. I was thinking about something that I really like right now which is something that people don't like because you're not supposed to like it, which is the badge invented by the guy who designed the "I <3 NY." He's invented another badge, "It's not warming it's dying," of which I have one.

It's black—there's a green earth suffused with blackness. And it has this nicely Gothic "oh god, I'm wearing a badge, how lame" thing going on. And people are picking it apart on the progressive but anthropocentric websites, saying, "oh, it's not dying, it's us who are killing these species, and you're destroying the belief in warming again because you're saying it's not warming, aha!" But the whole thing is, this is a badge, dude. This is something that you wear on your shirt. And immediately it has this slight lameness. It's not this horrific, great big "you must think this now, otherwise there's something wrong with you," you see. It's a badge. It's the most pathetic possible thing you could imagine. So in a funny way, wearing this badge is a badge of hyposubjectivity. And it's obviously a toy, too.

It's a toy. And the idea is very cute, and New Agey, and therefore interesting, because it's again perverse from a certain scholarly view. It is the hundredth monkey idea, which is that if enough people wear such a badge, everyone will start to care about earth. Which is charming and might even be true. Shall we end it there? And we'll pick it up at our next lunch?

Coda

But in a very real sense, isn't saying things in a half-assed halfway way precisely the very content of this project? Exactly. It is. And in this very retro way, too, like the madmen speaking into their dicta-phones. Thinking aloud as they go. The people in this restaurant are going, "what the fuck are they on?" "Oh, they're just doing their thing. They're just living their hyposubjective existence..."

II ooo, dasein, bananas, phenomenology, children's books, space movies, revolutionary infrastructure, micronauts

Off we go. Off we go again. Hyposubjects. So let's hear more about object-oriented ontology (OOO), and what the place of the subject is within it. If we're talking about hyposubjects, does that connect to the work of OOO or is this off on a new trajectory? And then a second issue: can we connect hyposubjects to phenomenology? In the phenomenological tradition, subjects are always very present, the necessary ego.

So the first issue is OOO and its notion of subject. I think what OOO would say would be that there's much less difference between what me, some kind of putative, dormant, or possibly representative, or bad photocopy of, or proxy for, or ridiculous parody of "the subject" does when he's thinking and talking about stuff, and what a bottle of kombucha is doing when it's sitting on a table. The kombucha is a hyposubject and mosquitoes are hyposubjects and somehow, ecology, politicswise, is all about shrinking down with all the other hyposubjects as it were. That's the intuitive connection. And this is where Graham Harman might get cross—I'm pretty sure he wouldn't, however (keep reading).

Quentin Meillassoux has accused Graham's view recently of being "subjectalism." In other words, we all know that subjects are extrinsic decorations on dead matter, that's Meillassoux's point. So what Graham is doing is saying that everything is a subject.

Also the Latourian move. Graham's worried about that, but I'm not so worried about that. I was talking to a Heideggerian in Rotterdam last year. He said, "Oh so what you're saying is that basically everything has Dasein." Whereas you see for Graham, it's almost like Dasein is such a weak category that nothing really has Dasein. For me, Dasein is weak, and that's why you can let bottle caps have it. The other thing Graham's worried about is panpsychism, the idea that everything has a soul or something like that. I'm not so squeamish on that point. I'm not convinced that what we're doing looks like some kind of Disney version of animism.

Now I know Graham would agree with me that Meillassoux's objection isn't much of one at all. If everything is a "subject" as Meillasoux claims Harman is saying, "subject" is a terribly cheap defanged thing that has no anthropocentric, patriarchal or racist bite to it, and kind of that means it's not really a subject at all, because of the ideological conditions in which the full-on concept of subject means something. That kind of supposedly transcendental being always seemed to hover like a halo over white boys' heads in particular.

If you let this lame "subject" hover over everything, as it were, it stops being a halo and just becomes the way an entity is always temporally displaced from itself (so-called "ek-static" being in Heidegger's terms). It becomes an entity's shadow, its vapor trail, its Duchamp Nude-Descending-a-Staircase quality. Its specter. In other words, thanks Meillassoux, you just gave the world proof that OOO is an un-alienated theory of the subject. The subject as such is alienated. That's the point here. A hyposubject is in a way someone who can tell they're intrinsically un-alienated, not because they're whole white boys underneath, or white boys made of glass (transparent boys), but because they know they have an essence that is like that of a banana.

What bananas are, their "essence" if you like, is the never-quite-arriving futurality of banana data. Data (it's in the word, it's a past participle) is the past. The form of a thing, its data, is what happened to it. A shrimp sandwich is a thing that happened to some shrimp. My face is a map of the acne that happened to it when I was nineteen. But what is this shrimp sandwich, what is this face all about, what are bananas anyway?

Think about it. When you bite a banana you obtain a banana bite. When you lick a banana you get a banana lick. When you think about a banana you get a banana thought. When you draw the banana you get a banana drawing. When the banana becomes sentient and goes on Oprah and starts to talk—"I found myself in a paragraph about bananas by the authors of *Hyposubjects*...it was a traumatic self-awakening..."—all you have is banana interview. Even the banana themselves can't fully access the banana banana. And since licking is just as good or just as bad as thinking at accessing the banana banana, snails and hurricanes are just as good or as bad as humans and there's nothing special about humans at all.

Note that this doesn't mean that hurricanes have the same rights as humans or whatever. Even if one suspects hurricanes think our Dasein is pretty weak too. It's a terrifically freeing way of thinking, politically. It means you're free to make the kinds of political affiliations you want to make, without recourse to metaphysics. You don't have to prove that lemurs have a self-concept or that angelfish are smart in order to forge solidarities with them. Let's get on with it!

That's a whole bunch of bananas. If you want to translate that into tarrying with the negative Hegel speak then go right ahead, be my guest!

One thing intrinsic to the word *hyposubject* and also the word *object* are that they imply terms borrowed from Aristotle that might be part of the problem. This idea of manipulable lumps versus manipulators. So how do you transcend that? Is everything just one? That's one solution. Or, are there no objects or subjects, just matter? Or, and this would be more like historical materialism or Foucauldianism but applied to everything, is it actually the case that relationality between things despite me and also with me is what makes the world go round? We don't have to make everything be one to get rid of the subject/object dualism. Instead we have a kind of duality at every place in the universe. That'd be my quick, intuitive response.

We'll need to talk about Husserl too. He's so important for un-transcendentalizing what we might mean by *subject*. Graham calls it object-oriented idealism. In other words, you're thinking of this salad. The salad there is an intentional object. In other words, it's not that thing. It's the salad in your mind. And so you are thinking in salad mode, or you're thinking in salad color—you're thinking saladly. Of course you can hope saladly, you can promise saladly and hate saladly. It's the basic Hegelian point, that everything, every idea, comes shrink-wrapped with an attitude towards it. And somehow these ideas are also "objects," or hyposubjects actually. They are entities—rather meme-like—they sort of live and run free in my head and I get to reproduce them, I get to be a vector for them. You get from one to the other—that is from Husserl to the OOO stuff—by subtracting the idea that a thinking or positing subject is making all this be, is making all this be real from some sort of privileged place. So you can have your Derrida, and you can have your Foucault, but with some kind of really twisted, modified realism.

OOO is a wonderful diagnosis of our contemporary, epistemic condition in that respect. More than that, I would posit that it has its own deep-seated phenomenological basis, too, both in the individuated Husserlian sense, necessarily, of an ego unified by its experiential flux and flow. But also in the sense of a more anthropologically or sociologically inflected phenomenological tradition, in which we have to considers networks of egos and the relations between them. And even Husserl very much allows the possibility of nonhuman egos. So those object-oriented ideal networks are filled with humans and nonhumans fluxing along with one another. This is long before anyone is talking about "ecophenomenology" mind you. It makes me think that all phenomenology is really ecophenomenology at its core.

A book we might talk about is *How Forests Think* as a side note to this. I just read it. Latour told me to. Latour's apparently very keen on it. I am wondering to what extent this book sends us back to a pre-Lévi-Strauss mode rather than pushing us to a post-Lévi-Strauss mode. In other words, might he have reinvented the wheel of immediate contact with nature? And might there be some rather scary things about that? In other words, I really love the idea of networks of things communicating indexically. Although I think there are ways things can communicate without even being indexical. But some of his examples are actually not indexical, they're much more hands-on physical than that. That idea I love by the way.

The trouble for me comes in the book's very rigidly defined life/non-life boundary. It's the difference between lying on your back where the jaguar's not going to kill you because you're face up, and lying on your side or your front where the jaguar is going to kill you because you're an object. So to prove to you that I'm a subject, I have to give you eye contact all the time. Which means that as soon as I lose eye contact you can treat me like Agamben's bare life. I'm potentially a Holocaust victim at any moment. I really enjoyed Kohn's work when I first encountered it. At that point it wasn't how forests think, but rather how dogs dream. I still remember the question that I asked him after his talk, which was along the lines of, "How do you account for the fact that this entire anthropology of life is itself a human knowledge project?

At what point in this account does that mediation surface and matter? You were just speaking of immediation and that was my concern then as well. Immediation, whether philosophical or political, often generates a naturalism to stabilize its ontological convictions. That naturalism in turn inoculates itself against contingency, historicity, whatever. This is not to equate Kohn with political essentialism but rather to say that the starry eyed embrace of life has its own circuit, its own fullness, and is thus very capable of anaesthetizing itself to its own political conditions of possibility. That's in a way what Beth Povinelli is saying in *Geontologies*. This is perhaps why the post-humanist literature often comes under attack for being apolitical—which I don't think it necessarily is—precisely because it has the same trouble most theory does of asking the reflexive question: under what circumstances does this project become epistemically intuitive and generative.

And what we are surfacing with concepts like hyperobjects and hyposubjects is not just a genealogy of thought. I'm skeptical of the model of great thinkers passing great ideas to each other over the centuries—it has never rung true to me. Instead these concepts, "hyperobjects" or "anthropology of life" or anything else for that matter are rooted in a particular moment, a particular environment, an ecology, an egology—here again the phenomenological line of thinking—all these conditions summon durable epistemic intuitions that can then and only then be mobilized conceptually. My question concerns why particular concepts come to circulate at specific times in specific contexts. In *Hyperobjects*, for example, we find global warming and the Anthropocene as conditions that are reconfiguring our thinking. One might also add conditions like the emergence of synthetic biology that truly cast aside nature/culture distinctions or nuclear weapons which are capable of voiding that and almost everything else. My point is that we don't generate new concepts as a matter of will or insight but rather because we are being infused by new forces and conditions and then at a certain point crystallize as concepts. The exciting thing about this moment is that there are so many new forces and conditions coming into being that it is remarkably epistemically generative.

I am thinking of all the positive, vital intellectual energy that has become attached to anti-anthropocentric projects now. We come to comprehend this reality through negation. And in turn the spread of negation is amounting to a zeitgeist-level or episteme-level shift in northern philosophy. That's a good thing as long as it feeds the many projects—creative projects, political projects, relational projects—all the projects that seek for themselves an ending of the Anthropocene or a new trajectory.

No doubt. A concept like hyposubject might also solve something with regard to biopolitics. With the view that the forest is a hyposubject, I don't have to prove to you that it's alive so you can preserve it. I don't have to say "alive means you can't chop it down and dead means definitely go ahead and chop it down." In other words, a hyposubject might not be definable as living or dead actually. There's a total category shift that prevents the—in the end biopolitical actually—arguments and dispositifs that get all of this stuff into a snarl right now. If the forest is a hyposubject made of other hyposubjects—like a marriage for example, you know, this wisdom in the U.S. tax code that treats married people as one and a half people. The whole is actually less than the sum of its parts.

That's always true so that a frog is also less than the sum of its parts. This might be a nice little set theory definition of hyposubjects: a hyposubject is an entity that is less than the sum of its parts. But back to Kohn, I have this rule, I never go after people, but rather just use the thoughts inside them and then expand, rather than...Exactly! Do we want to invest our energy in arguing who has the best concepts? I think the situation is far too urgent for that. Fencing over concepts was a luxury we had back in the Holocene.

Kohn's done something very interesting, getting a bunch of scholars to think about how forests might be alive, which is something that was once restricted to a Sunday afternoonish daydreaming. So good for him. But I have no issue with critical engagement for the purposes of clarifying what a line of thinking, namely ours, is. It feels to me like it is a different wavelength from where we are, not better or worse, just different.

Did I mention I saw an interview with Jón Gnarr. With Craig Ferguson, is it? The talk show host. Not Niall Ferguson, the irritating historian. From the Late Late Show? Yeah. He's rather feisty, and Jón's much more subtle humor was a little bit steamrolled by the talk show host who inevitably, always in the end, wants to appear to have one over on his show guests. Nevertheless, Jón said something really fantastic, which was, "Remember how the mammals survived the dinosaur's asteroid? They were really small. And they crawled." Wow, that's a direct connection.

No mistake. And on that note, I brought along this book. (The book in question is placed between them) Let's talk about it. It's called If by David Smith, illustrated by Steve Adams. And there's another one, but I couldn't find it on the bookshelf called something like Tiny Creatures: The Wonderful World of Microbes. But this will do for starters. Because it's a kid's book for pretty much all ages. And, as you see, there are these little whimsical illustrations that look like maps, kind of silhouette-y Jan Pienkowski-like. They have a slightly Gothic quality to them. And you see they're very ordinary. He's using pencils, and I'm assuming—what's that stuff? It's not gouache. It's the other thing that you rub...

Pastels? Pastels, right. And he's using dinner plates like, "If the Milky Way galaxy was shrunk to the size of dinner plate, our whole solar system would be smaller than this speck of dust too small to see." The reason why I brought it in was that it strikes me as something of a symptom of how humans digest nonhuman scales. When you go to the many scale toys that you can go on the internet, or in the basement of the Natural Science Museum, and you can go from planck length to the size of the universe in a couple of seconds.

There is a kind of scientistic "I'm outside the universe, laughing or terrified" quality to it that is politically very disempowering, while at the same time giving one a feeling of total power. Like in the way that you can stroll through a Mahler symphony on iTunes with just one swift move. Of course when you actually listen to it it's devastatingly powerful and affects your emotions, but you can turn it off with a click. But you see these kids' illustrations are friendly, yet disturbing, designed for kids and parents to understand and marvel at nonhuman scales. And I just thought, this is interesting because, in terms of the kind of relationality you're talking about, this is humans acting like hyposubjects. They're making a children's book. Children's books are a minor genre in the Deleuzean sense. You can say things in them that are still taboo to say in grownups' books. And some of this information is just dazzling. I don't want to say they're propaganda. That's the sort of thing one could only say about children's books if one accepts a really really passive model of children—

That they're always pedagogical in some way. But this clearly has a profoundly nonpedagogical aspect. We're looking at this page called "Inventions through Time," and there's this kind of swirling piece of something that looks like a spring onion with computers and laptops and wheels and things hanging off it, and these are all humanity's inventions. Going back and back through human history to fire, and how there's been this explosion right here. And sure, you're getting informed, but there's also a kind of completely nonfunctional disturbance happening. It's kind of whimsically kitschy. It's not officially odd. This one was amazing to me. This is "The History of Life on Earth," where you've basically got bacteria and then you've got blank blank blank, then suddenly, Cambrian explosion. Pow! And before that just blank, like there's nothing. Mind-blowing.

It's something that you probably couldn't see so well using one of those scale toys. Because the scale toys are great for machismo, like oh look, universe—planck—universe—planck. But going through the middle a bit, where there are so many layers of granularity and so many hyposubjects as it were, you can't really do that with them. Or at least I don't. You know the way this would be presented in a corny book that you buy in the natural science museum, the type with lots of flashy photographs from NASA, and immediately you've got the scientistic alienation going on again. Whereas here we've got different species. We've got these silhouettes, the Pienkowski Goth-type silhouettes, and then we've got these kind of silhouette-y beings, and this tree that they're springing off of. You can see how—if all life was a tree—these would be the animals and these are the fungi. There are this many species of protozoa. And that's really extraordinary because going back a few pages, they existed in this enormous ocean of blank. By themselves for so long.

And it's giving you the feeling of dizzy but through ordinary household objects. So ordinary objects start to evoke the dizziness instead of the familiarity. Anyway, I just thought it was really neat. A kind of scalar uncanny. And we both thought last time that teen or tween lit might also be a place where one might find hope. Haven't done any homework on that. I'm still working my way through this kid's book. I may be more sensitized to what's going on there because of our teenager but things like *The Hunger Games* or *Attack on Titan* have become pop cultural phenomena unto themselves. There's more to be said about both of them. But I want to say that I find this If book really effective. Leaving aside for a moment the design of it and the intentionality of this type of a project—how it explores the dizzying, unsettling dimension of scale, is really effective and affective. It speaks to a coming-to-terms-with moment. For the designer/producer/artist of the book, for the child reading this and the parent reading it to the child. It's a very gentle way to try to introduce a new set of aesthetic organs into the hyperobjective, hyposubjective world in which we live.

Of course all domestic objects are the product of billions of years of evolution and global scale problems, such as industry, capital, you know the usual, boring, but very real, kind of David Harvey where-did-your-breakfast-come-from sort of question. So when I read this book I just thought, wow. This is the first one I've seen but I bet you there's a bunch now coming out of the woodwork. It's very honest, it's very humble. It mirrors the dislocatedness of political discourse or economic discourse. But those are precisely the types of machines of truth-making that cannot reveal their vulnerability and simplicity. They need to remain constantly enshrouded.

Look at this bit here, there's a whole politics of water! I've never seen that in a children's book before. There's all kinds of stuff about 'preserve the animals' but I've never seen—And this is great, too. Because here you have the titan figure and the hyposubject figure...

Yeah! Sorry to interrupt. It's just really apropos to what we were saying. This waiter, he's also a part of a larger corporate machine that's swamping you with this. With a smiley face. It's perfect. It's so subtle. Just this image alone shows you how the hyperobject has both its singular monophasic form here as the titanic waiter as well as its plural multiphasic form of the infinitude of cups of water. They stand in contrast to each other, but also in contrast to the small children dangling from lines, being marionetted here, almost. As we said last time, the hyperobject, or the recognition of the hyperobject, demands parallel recognition of the hyposubject. They exist in a relational formation. And they're playing. They could be trapped hanging on for dear life, but they also could be using those ropes, somehow, to negotiate their way around, perhaps to subvert it.

The constant appearance of play suggests that this moment isn't just about the darkest images and concepts we are capable of conjuring. Hyposubjectivity doesn't have to be the situation of being hunted by predatory forces, whether it's capital or global warming. Rather, there's an opening with the recognition of hyposubjects to—at least at the human end of the ecology of hyposubjects—to question what it means for us humans to be bifurcated now into the hypersubjective titan form on the one hand, epitomizing all that aspires to the global, literally the titans of industry and modernity. And we are now realizing that our titan form has accomplished a particular path of acceleration toward planetary extinction, a Hegelian drive to negate everything you wish to possess. Whereas on the other hand, there is a new sort of potential human that's being awakened here that hasn't figured out what it can do yet or what its responsibilities and entitlements and ethics can be—but what it does know is that it is not the mega. That one certainty of identification: "that's not me."

And so we're playing. We're playing, trying to understand. Yes, and the notion of the human that the antihumanism is quite rightly assaulting—it's not a face on the sand. It's a face on the gigantic water corporations. The humanization of that, which is as you say is an extinction logistics reaching a kind of almost perfect functioning, that if left to continue, would within the next hundred years quite happily wipe out 50% of all life forms on the planet. Humans too would be part of that. Relatedly, we have to keep in mind the status of the extraterrestrial, our investment in the extraterrestrial, as the corollary of all this terrestrial havoc wreaking.

This is *Melancholia* smashing into earth. And Lars von Trier, at least in that movie, is, from my point of view, with the bad guys. If ever there was a hyposubject, it's the distressed mother who drives around and around hopelessly in her SUV trying to find a way out with her kids. Kirsten Dunst is all good and everything, but she's got plasma coming out of her fingers. It's the meaningless ritual on the edge of the end. And isn't it also true that the implication of her kind of speculative realism, which is that 'there is no other life in the universe'—she says it quite explicitly, 'I know things'—is that literally melancholia? Which you could feel when confronted with gigantic-mega. How do you get out from that? That's the whole project of this book. So, as gorgeous as that film is, one of its problems is that it's stuck in Wagnerian misogyny.

Those opening "Tristan" chords that are part of the whole thing are the ultimate, horrible Wagnerian chords of yearning desire. This idea that there's something intrinsically horrible about it, or intrinsically tragic, strikes me as being a patriarchal and therefore also agrilogistical construct. That all your desires will never really work because they've always already been co-opted by some kind of disaster. Think about the end of—to take another sci-fi image that I find really disturbing—Philip K. Dick's *A Scanner Darkly*. Where you pan out, he's in—and it's very obvious in the movie—this giant field made of flowers. They don't smell, taste, they don't even have a noticeable psychoactive effect. It's just that they have the psychoactive effect of cynicism, actually. You get to watch yourself watching yourself watching yourself watching yourself. And yet you're always caught in the mega-corporation somehow. As attractive as it is to go through that moon tunnel, that's the kind of adult sci-fi where you're like 'oh, I'm grown up now, I don't want stuff like—(aside: what did we see the other day?) The Virgin.' Which has all kinds of issues with it, but nevertheless has a happy ending of some kind. 'Oh that's just naïve. That's for kids. I watch the relentless doom.'

That somehow what you should be doing, as an adult, with your pleasure—is reducing it to patriarchy, basically. It all comes down to that. And the way that Kirsten Dunst—it's actually not Kirsten Dunst, I can't remember the name—but then she subverts everything just for the sake of subverting. So that in a sense she's part of the machine. And again, I feel like, if it was me and it is me—because global warming is descending—I'm not sitting here, trying to find some kind of Zen space. I'm running around screaming. I think that's much more realistic and true to hyposubjects.

While you were thinking of that, I was thinking of the Cuarón film, *Gravity*. It opens with the technomodernist idyll, like *2001*, the beautiful white equipment and astronauts floating out in space. For a moment everything has been mastered but it's only an illusion. Suddenly the whole apparatus is shredded, also beautifully, by a chain of human actions gone awry. The extraterrestrial is suddenly revealed again as a human-swallowing abyss and there is a desperate attempt to return to mother earth, through enormous effort. One character escapes in a sense by travelling off into space, never to be recovered.

But that's also a kind of perfect extinction fantasy, having sacrificed oneself to save another and then to unite with the deep inky infinite. The other character, who is also a hyposubject, has to become a bricoleuse and fight her way back to earth using the scraps and remains of what's left above earth. All that effort, only to return to the water again, the origin of terrestrial life. It's like Fight Club for the Anthropocene, a battle within the self to reunite with the planet. And she has visions of the other astronaut, the importance of allowing yourself to hallucinate, which is not accepted. Yes. All important.

The other similarity with the von Trier film is comedy. They use Sandra Bullock, and they've got her basically in slapstick mode, at high altitude. Likewise we're supposed to laugh at the mother in *Melancholia* because she's driving around and say, 'look at how stupid that is. She can't escape.' She's like a rat in a maze, and there's a Bergsonian contempt—she's being reduced to a machine. But everything is that. Everything is a kind of a puppet or, not even a puppet, of forces you can't control, but just caught in its own style somehow. This is a Bergsonian thing, you can't have a thought outside of the style. So, it strikes me, and this is something that obviously our friend Jón would like, that comedy is the underside of *Gravity*. And then I wonder how *Moon* fits in actually. Because in *Moon* we've got an actual corporate product, un-corporatizing itself, getting into one of the pods that sends—whatever that is, hydrogen?—and returning itself to earth.

And in there we find the abject version of itself, who, unlike Clooney disappearing into the darkness, actually allows the healthier version to reinsert him into the tank, and just slowly die of cold and pneumonia. He's a hyposubject, isn't he? They're all hyposubjects. And the sick version of him becomes the hero whose sacrifice somehow enables the other guy. The first duty of the prisoner is to escape. I like those stories where from the first moment you see the lead character who is trying to escape from his or her situation. And as soon as you see them jumping rope, you know that they're going to get off the planet somehow. *Moon* is a great example. And I'm sure there are others too in the same genre. On the one hand, this isn't the *Star Trek* era, which was a wonderfully Keynesian, modernist, endless growth, endless prosperity, endless mastery sort of modeling. At least in its first go round. And then later with the *Next Generation* and *Deep Space 9* it becomes more about trade and capital, absorbing the neoliberal atmosphere. This era is different from both of those, space figures differently, and perhaps there is a nostalgia for *Star Trek* for just that reason.

Our fantasy life won't tolerate a mastered vision of space anymore since fantasies have to have enough anchorage in the real in order to operate effectively as fantasies. It's fascinating to me that our space fantasies now are not about traveling to distant galaxies light-years away, but rather remain painfully close to earth in orbits that are very troubled. Like in *Melancholia* something is coming for us. Here then is our second hypothesis. The first one was that a hyposubject is always less than the sum of its parts. The second one is that a hyposubject is an extraterrestrial in some sense. An exohuman seeking a home. An exohuman, lovely.

Not descending from on high, but desperately scrambling back with what weird little boxes and gizmos you can crunch together. The bricoleur. Making do with what's available. Exactly. Another one is *Elysium*. It's a bad movie with a great premise. Whereas *District 9*, which was the same director I believe, was a more consistent and wonderfully grotesque allegory. That one's best known for using the extraterrestrial as a vehicle to critique racism and apartheid. But I actually found the eventual synthesis of the human and the nonhuman in *District 9* interesting from our perspective. Anyway, here's what I found compelling about *Elysium*: humanity has developed these marvelous biopolitical technologies, including machines that will cure any ailment and guarantee endless life. But of course only the rich have access to them. And they decide rather than reform the earth, they're going to build this orbital colony. Meanwhile down on earth, it's a *Bladerunner* scenario. Worse actually. *Bladerunner* meets *Thunderdome*, desperate working conditions, radiation exposure, short life span—in short a biopolitical nightmare. So we don't want to be on earth...

Exactly. But we don't get very far away either, interestingly. In our fantasies of the extraterrestrial now we're always being sucked back, or, like Matt Damon in *Elysium* having to sacrifice our lives to help our fellow hyposubjects...We should also talk about this book *Sapiens*, which is doing the rounds right now. More in Europe, because it hasn't come out yet in the States, but it's basically the kind of thing that I find aggravating yet satisfying. It's not unlike my argument, but without the philosophy. History has a tendency to proceed as a discipline based on prepackaged theoretical constructs that are unexamined. So, you know: 'human beings evolved, and made all the other ones extinct'—slight issue with that—'big rig agriculture'... 'Anthropocene'...'there will be two classes of people: there will be rich people who can do anything to anything, including their own bodies, and poor people who can't.' It's like technofix plus doom. Transhumanist but actually humanist.

That's the ultimate dream of the old school humanism: I can keep on transcending myself. The author's saying, it's going to be that without end, maybe with a spinoff that we could solve some problems on earth. That's where I think: I never want to be in that future. Speaking empirically, poor people can find themselves married to people who run oil corporations, at least in this town. Capitalism itself is quite fungible, for humans. Because it's very rationalist: 'I've broken it down to mustard and ketchup. You can have mustard or you can have ketchup. That's your choice. You can have extension or you can have the soul.' There are a lot of assumptions in there. There's an assumption that human beings make other entities go extinct, just by existing. And that, becoming more and more powerful than ourselves, than we are now, may not be preferable, but is somehow inevitable.

This synoptic view is really why satire was number one on the charts in the eighteenth century. This catastrophe, where you're standing on top of the mountain looking down on these poor saps in the city, that's your mode of satire. There are all these poems by

Pope and Johnson where they look down on the whole of humanity and proclaim, what a mess. I worry that if ecological discourse means progressing into an ever more democratic future with an eighteenth-century way of picturing things, not adjusting to the Anthropocene and the philosophy that weirdly goes along with it, then I don't want to be a part of that class. In other words, *Sapiens*. The word itself, suggesting that the human is what he is thinking: canny, wise—that's why we beat the Neanderthals. It's an old-school story: 'we were able to see around corners that they couldn't see around.' Maybe we just had sex with them so many times that they're indistinguishable from us. What about that for a nice idea?

Why does it have to be about destroying? That's not survival of the fittest. Survival of the fittest is much more hyposubjective. It's, 'I managed to pass on my genome before I died. I had an orgasm in a certain context once in my life.' At some point we'll want to talk about our epistemic zeitgeist and also to reckon with some of these hyperobjective concepts like 'the market' and 'the economy'. Much of that critical work has been done elsewhere, we don't have to go on and on about it. But such concepts are also part of the situation we live in, a certain phase of globalization. In the eighteenth century, they may have been talking about the human, but practically speaking what they were on about were Europeans. Oh, exactly.

Mostly Europeans of a certain class and gender. Because Europeans, no matter where they live, they get to live on top of a mountain. I was just reading John Stuart Mill, and liberty sounds very wonderful until you realize that children don't get it, that women probably won't get it, and that everyone living outside civilized Europe gets "benevolent despotism." Mill worked for the British East India Company by the way. Children get it another way, by being forced into chimneys, forced into machines.

Yes. So there is an era that produces these discourses on the human, on liberty, on freedom. And these are very much the engines of the beginnings of what becomes today's order, already naturalizing violence and inequity. There's a deep correlation between that and the social Darwinism that was weirdly in the air before Darwin even published his thing.

If we have time for one last line of thought, I was going to tell you a bit about something I've been working on, a paper on infrastructure—again a theme for our times. Infrastructure is not an analytic that immediately attracted me, so I had to think my way into it a bit. But I became interested in the relationship between infrastructure and revolution. And I came to think that what we need is a new form of revolutionary infrastructure. Because the old revolutionary infrastructure, both philosophical and material, everything that's associated with the revolutionary programs which flourished between the mid-nineteenth and mid-twentieth centuries—you know, Leninism, Bolshevism, Marxism, Maoism—these were all wedded to mega-level industrial programs, needing mega-levels of energy to power enormous productive apparatuses, like Lenin's equation that Communism = the Soviets + electrification. And the mass industrial use of energy is what we know now is huge factor in our current dilemma. Industrial fueled abundance is an apparatus of mega, what's putting the hyper in the hyperobject. So we need new infrastructure.

But we also need to believe that there's a possibility of revolution that is not of the mega kind but perhaps which is itself hyposubjective. But what would a hyposubjective revolutionary infrastructure look like? To go back to our discussion of squatting, it's not about the globalized proletariat seizing back the mass apparatus of use value production, so much as it is pervasive creative squatting within the grid/pipeline/road world—this infrastructure bequeathed to us by capitalist modernity—and disabling them, link by link from the inside, while repurposing their materials.

Flash, flash, flash. I have a flash on that. So we've got two hypotheses, and one political injunction which is to squat, and maybe the next political injunction of the hyposubject, the next rule of how to play at being a hyposubject is to play and to squat. And not to cease control. It's grab. Grab the energy through it and—

Tap it. Make your own infrastructure. Tap it. Build your own pathetic little device that everybody can laugh at because it's not going to change the world. But now you're off the grid. That's another injunction: become your own infrastructure. I was thinking about Hermann Scheer, the guy who was more or less the architect of Germany's renewable energy transition and a radical thinker in a Social Democratic Party long removed from radical politics. He has this marvelous argument that so much of our thinking is warped by the long inefficient supply chains of fossil and nuclear energy that empower centralized governments but force the rest of us to pay rent for their inefficiencies. Meanwhile the thing about solar energy—solar meaning solar but also wind, biomass, etc.—is that their supply chains are much shorter. They don't need a centralized grid infrastructure to operate, in fact they don't work best in a grid world. They have a different material politics which could enable a different human politics to emerge. Right now grid engineers hate solar energy because they see it as parasitic and weird and intermittent.

They view renewable energy as a virus in the grid world, endangering the health and stability of the system. And it is! As more and more new energy projects tap and hack into the grid world, creating their own autonomies and power circuits, it dawns on us that the grid doesn't matter so much any more. It's not needed. I remember how, back in the day—when going to Glastonbury Festival was the most important thing you could do as a teenager—having your own generator, if you were in a band, was the most important thing you could have. So there was this guy, called Generator John, and his claim to fame was that he owned a generator. And so he went around to all the bands with his generator—yeah, it ran off oil—but the point is that they had own their own house, they could do their own gigs. So you know, 'get your own generator,' could be a slogan. You know, generate yourself.

I think so. I just wanted to say that part of the unthinkability of moving against the trajectory of the Anthropocene is this idea that we must always continue to supply the grid. You know: 'wind won't work because it's too intermittent for the grid, and solar won't work because it's too weak for the grid. We need oil, we need coal, we need thermoelectric power plants running on fossil fuels.' This is precisely the sleight of hand. A way of always slipping the mega back into it, of reinforcing the hypersubject-hyperobject death drive loop.

It's revolution in the same way that if you were to take a pair of pliers and really bend part of the shape in one corner, it could be revolution, a new thing. Rather than seizing the entire thing, chucking it into the fire, and then replacing it with the same thing, pretty much, from an infrastructural point of view. That's the problem with Marxist-Leninism. It wants the fires to burn just as brightly as before.

Because it remains anthropocentric philosophy there, a kind of Hegelianism where you say, 'go to the top level, which is the totality decides, and then you change the totality, then everything will be different at successively lower levels.' Whereas this idea of revolution is much more about what happens in the base, if you want to use that language. I'm thinking of this as a kind of retrofitting, about disassembling these apparatuses, but maybe still getting to use some of the parts.

And think of the way that gets denigrated in the later twentieth-century Academy as a hippie, incorrect, unthinkable, unspeakable solution. The most grant money, or at least the most pages in the *London Review of Books*, is going to go to the guy who's saying 'complete change of everything.' And now that we're faced with an actual, physical complete change of everything, the idea that we could get on top of it feels disastrous. I mean, what? We're going to allow geoengineering to fill the ocean with iron filings? We're going to let that happen? You know, how's that been working out? So this is the bit in the book when we sound really apolitical, from the point of view of the teenaged selves that we once were. It's basically a rejection of a certain kind of politics, in this case, the deeply problematic contradictions in the kind of revolutionary politics that we grew up with in the Cold War. But I don't want to give up on revolutionary politics.

Perhaps the neo-anarchist movements of today are on a similar wavelength: I think what we are saying intersects with some aspects of their thinking. But we also have to imagine what could happen to these mega structures, over time, through pervasive hyposubjective action. We have to recognize that this so-called mega is always already composed of hyposubjects. Hyposubjects are already acting out everywhere all the time—what else have we been talking about?—the question is how to orchestrate a hyposubjective occupation and dispossession of the Anthropocene apparatus. That seems to me the political challenge. When I was a kid there were these Japanese toys called micronauts. And they were transparent-colored humanoids with silver heads. I like the idea of micronauts versus mega world. Hyposubjects. Micronautical voyages.

Finding the militant edge of hyposubjectivity to push things forward. And maybe micronauts are militant hyposubjects. Wow! We've got so many—! Let's hear it for the micronauts everywhere.

III global village, dyslocation, right wing fantasies, finance capital, speculative realism, downloads, bliss-horror, role-playing games

So where are we now? We were wondering about the atavistic fictional right-wing regression to a moment in which Britain is no longer a part of Europe, fueled by racist fantasies about immigration. What is it all really about? Above and beyond reactions to neoliberalism. Let's tell the story this way: it was fun, maybe, in the 1990s, especially if you were a global telecommunications company, to think about the idea that everyone's connected.

Those utopian adverts where African people were waving at you have now become—well, the reality of "globality" is very depressing and very disturbing and very inhibiting in political speech because everyone is trying to say the right thing all the time. And trying to hypercorrect their policy in a kind of Oedipal guilt death spiral of political will. But, beyond that, it's about all of us realizing that we're a species, which is tantamount to realizing that you're a bit of a fingernail of a zombie that's just reacting without any consciousness. And that disturbs at least 200 years of philosophy, and also 300 or 400 years of ideology. We are no longer living in a world in which we can say 'I'm in the local right now as opposed to the global. I'm in a place vs. space. I'm here, which is in the middle of everywhere.' So what's happened actually is that this supposed abstract global has turned into another kind of local, only really, really big. I was saying this at Northwestern a couple of weeks ago. Somebody was wondering what happens to place.

The corny thing would be to say 'well, there's no place anymore. It's all been eaten away by space.' But in a way it's the opposite. The soothing idea that I'm surrounded by abstract eternity infinity space, which is a box in which I'm contained, is no longer thinkable. In fact, we're here, and we're also on Earth. And Earth is not Mars. It has this atmosphere and it has this biosphere and it has these beings on it, for instance, the human species. We've got eyes. We like to turn on car engines. We have this kind of temporality structure and not that one, and on and on and on. So, in other words, this supposed abstract 'anything could happen really,' even though I'm restricted locally, has completely and utterly crashed at this point. And the crash has come, ironically enough, through a greater amount of global connectivity between humans. So that it is a global village, in a way, but not in that nice, utopian-sounding way, like when it might have occurred to people that they wanted to teach the world to sing in perfect harmony and buy the world a bottle of Coca-Cola back in the early 70s.

That was never McLuhan's global village, right? McLuhan's global village had frightful dystopian potential too. It was really all about this idea that the servomechanisms of electric communication were externalizing human brain functions. To the extent that we developed, for lack of a better word, a global brain or an axonal-dendritic network that flashed images and ideas around the world with blinding speed. There was immense circulation and flow but also a kind of scalar disruption between the biotic human entity—the individual moving through linear time that McLuhan said was produced by print culture—and this globally enabled or extended, as he put it, humanity that sounds very cyborg-like even if that wasn't his language.

We're living proof of the dark side of that vision. What's collapsed is the idea that we are here and there is there—the anthropocentrism. That we're in a world where we are everywhere has been unmasked. It's in Einstein, isn't it? Euclidean space-time is a just a convenient scale for carrying on. We've sort of half known that for a while. There have been postmodern ways of saying what we're saying right now. But now is when it really happens. There's something that's really disturbing about it that, if you're a certain type of person, makes you want to retreat into a right-wing fantasy space.

There's a wonderful book written by an anthropologist named Doug Holmes called *Integral Europe*. He interviewed European right wing political leaders like Derek Beackon and Jean-Marie Le Pen, analyzed them, picked through their racism. What the book does a great job of surfacing is the welfarist fantasies that anchor their type of nationalism. The attempt to build a nice stable little fantasy home and hearth in the middle of a torrent of finance capital, multinational corporations, new kinds and intensities of people and value moving through the world in the 1990s. Dislocations multiply. Maybe the Euclidean worldview just can't be sustained anymore. If you look at the postmodern theory of the 1990s, it channels that same phenomenology of dislocatedness.

In a way, what we're dealing with is, not dislocation, but mallocation, the idea that location is a little bit sinister. My locatedness isn't good. It's all dislocation but this dislocation is dys-location. It's not that I find myself nicely cozily here, and then it's all disrupted. It's that I find myself rather sinisterly here. I'm on a planet. And it's this planet and not that planet. And this planet retroactively affects all its sub-regions. So one of the problems for the hyposubject is this feeling of dyslocation. In a funny way, in the postmodern discourse, there's a utopian thrill of 'oh finally, I'm disappearing into the bliss of not being the bourgeois subject or the Enlightenment subject.' Meanwhile, the Enlightenment subject is the cozy warm one. And it does deeply affect pleasure. It obviously affects political discourse, because people find it very difficult to speak in the way Jón Gnarr speaks, which is, 'I don't know what you're talking about. I need to go and study it and get back to you.' Of course that's what we need to be doing, because we can't understand it.

And we also need to have faith in the people who do understand some things better than we do, because we simply can't understand everything. That opposes the conventional populism, which has the attitude: 'the world is ontologically is what we intuitively perceive or morally feel it ought to be.' Then we behave as though that were fact. There's Nigel Farage for you, who seems to be somewhat of an improvement on his ilk we have over here. Oh my god. I'm not sure. That voice. We hear voices too and they're not as sophisticated.

Of course we do. Strangely enough, Farage's voice is ever so slightly subtly Americanized. He has the voice of a host of a 1950s variety show/ Americanized form of working-class entertainment. So his appeal is not really about being English; he's more like Sarah Palin. He's sprung from the fantasy world of Mrs. Thatcher, which is in turn some Americanized 50s fantasy space, which doesn't really have to do with traditional ideas of Englishness. Let me suggest something provocative to you: these people—the Palins, the Farages—are themselves engaging in a kind of speculative realism. I agree.

It's not conservative thinking because the discourse of work of these hallucinatory populists always turns on a speculative process of reimagining the real such that their politics makes any sense at all. What's amazing is that they can get so many people enrolled in their imaginative projects. There's some kind of eroticism caught up in it... Maybe this is more Derek Beackon than it is Nigel Farage but one fantasy is the apotheosis of the industrial working-class neighborhood. See, that wouldn't be Farage. The BNP is almost quaint—in a way, Farage is more like Hitler than the BNP. Because copying Hitler is already not quite being Hitler. That kind of appeal to a traditional working class neighborhood, that kind of skinhead vibe, it's more like lower middle class, car salesman, Darrell Issa world. That's what one hears in his voice with one's absurd English class radar. One hears the world of twitching curtains and a kind of know-nothing middle class-ness. Petit bourgeois. Which one assumes is the Hitler family background—rather disgruntled middle class people, as opposed to actual working class people seeking some kind of solidarity.

That's a good distinction. This is where location becomes the site of speculative fantasy. This idea of locatedness. The locatedness can be the hearth, it can be the home, it can be the neighborhood, it can be the city, it can be the nation. What was interesting about the BNP is that while their discourse contained a certain nationalist language, what they were really proud of was that they were knocking on doors and knew everyone's name on a given street. Their locatedness was street level. One almost has nostalgia for the good old days when one knew where one was with the BNP.

This conversation's taken a strange turn already.

Fascists just aren't how they used to be. Which might be a symptom of the emergence of the hyposubject and global dyslocation. Even fascism has to change so that it isn't about blood and soil. It's about some kind of weird smell of leather and a barbecue in a rainy suburban town. That doesn't mean it's nicer. I want to hold onto the idea that we are able to grasp certain dimensions of our present dyslocatedness. And one of them is finance capital, which has done much to erode a sense of security and location. When an entire country's currency can be taken down by speculators in Wall Street or London, that's the sort of thing that's only comprehensible to people in idioms of magic or religion. Finance is a kind of a hyperobject in a way.

Absolutely it is. That's an interesting subtheme actually, because thinking it as a hyperobject involves thinking it as extremely physically embodied. There are lots of capitalisms everywhere that are really embodied and local. Indeed, dys-local. And since you brought up telecommunications... For the most part, neoliberal movement in the U.S. neglected the great public infrastructures that the New Deal built—the roads, the bridges, the dams—all these mobility and energy infrastructures that a certain mode of nation-statehood was built upon. But neoliberal governance invested rather heavily in global telecommunications infrastructure and the Internet, which in turn created the possibility for finance as hyperobject.

Of course, finance capital has aspired to universalize itself for centuries. But these new infrastructures enabled it to reach some semblance of that reach and speed—speed!— where value can move like light and where rents can be acquired on transactions everywhere and where effects are scattered seemingly at random, completely mutant and unplanned and unimaginable. Thus somehow all the currency crashes and investment bubbles and odious debt become like the weather. Does one blame a hurricane for the destruction it wreaks? No, it's an "act of god." In its hyperobjectivity, finance becomes like "nature." The churning of these Sorcerer's apprentive algorithmic brooms as only the past, within nanoseconds of the "present," now that powerful servers control stock trades, but still the past. What is required is a political orientation towards the future.

It's not that the local has died. It's that the local has metastasized and that the universal has died in a way, or is in a very serious condition. And a symptom might be, this party, this UKIP, which doesn't have a platform. It only has the platform of 'we want to get out of Europe.' And everything else is pure aesthetics. Which again is weirdly evocative of what Benjamin doesn't like about fascism.

And the other strange thing is they want to get rid of Eastern Europeans, they want to deport them. Or at least some members of UKIP are saying that, much to the horror of the organizers. What no one's saying at all is, why is that not tantamount to saying that black and brown people should be repatriated? Is this actually a universal claim? Is it like ethnic cleansing or pogrom or a Holocaust? Or is it actually as absurd as fearing 'we're going to get all the Eastern Europeans?' Is there in fact no big picture at all? And why on Earth is that politically effective at this point? Again, I'm agreeing that there's a sort of horrible metastasis of the local and neoliberalism would be an example of it. Such that the tools that we've got for imagining a post-neoliberal future might be incorrect tools. Tools based on the past.

If we were to port this discussion over to the United States and think about immigration as a political problem, you'd find many resonances too. On the one hand, there's an effort to maintain the image of a bounded ethnos, an ethnological community. On the other hand, it's obvious we're living in a porous migrant society. Whether at the top, the middle or the bottom of the class hierarchy, all sorts of specialized labor are being brought in, whether it's technology specialists or people to pick fruits and vegetables. Nevertheless as in Europe you have an increasing appetite for these fantasies of national purity and extra-national invasive species. The realism of ethnological society is fantasy, but to the extent that a lot of people believe in the fantasy, one must take it seriously from a political perspective. It's a certain kind of real.

What if you were a Lacanian? Which thank god I'm not. You might end up saying that the way we imagine the Real is a disturbingly compelling, absurd image, as exemplified by the horror movie monster. The imaginary of the real, as opposed to how we symbolize the real or how we realize the symbolic—you know, this weird triangle—is excessive, absurd, irrational, monstrous. Perhaps one of the ways in which it manifests is in the absolutely groundless asceticism of the Tea Party and the UKIP. If they were to connect the dots and notice that LARPing in 1775 clothing is tantamount to saying that you want a world without free black people, they'd be deeply upset. They wouldn't say, 'Yes, that's exactly right. I'm dressing up like this, with my völkisch lederhosen equivalent.' This is why it's odd, because presumably the German fantasy was precisely that. So it is a quasi-fascist aesthetic, but inhabited by people who, when confronted with their racism, might become very upset. And weirdly then, somebody like Steve King can talk about boys with muscles the size of cantaloupes dragging an absurd amount of marijuana across the desert—75 lbs he says, which would fill, I don't even know, 75 lbs of pot would fill an entire building. So you have 130 lb boys with muscles the size of cantaloupes imagined to be dragging buildings worth of pot across the desert. It is an absolutely absurd image that shouldn't make any sense to anybody.

And yet somehow he feels empowered to imagine it and say it. This is what we're talking about: speculation. In a way, it is weirdly similar to the way that some speculative realist philosophy imagines reality as an absurd irrational monster that is about to devour (or which has just devoured) you. Apropos of our previous conversation about children's literature and teen literature I wanted to note an apparent teen enthusiasm for certain types of speculative realist projects. For example, there's this podcast *Welcome to Night Vale*. Have you heard of it? Oh, no.

It's been on for a few years now. Sort of H.P. Lovecraft meets Garrison Keillor. The premise being that these are news reports from a small town somewhere in the Southwest in which all conspiracy theories turn out to be real. It's worth listening to. It captures something of the hyposubjective-hyperobjective Zeitgeist. Then there's another one, a popular webcomic called *Homestuck* done in MS Paint. It's very lo-fi, cool media. But it's about a group of kids who install the beta for a game called Sburb and installing the game brings down meteors that destroy the Earth even as they are uploaded into the game environment, which takes place on a series of other planets. So by playing Sburb the actual suburban home life is annihilated, the digital download becomes a portal to extraplanetary adventure. It has a huge fandom.

The downloading process has its precedent with *Videodrome*. As soon as you switched on the television set, the alien entity—whatever that is—uploads itself into your head. Or with *The Ring* and the telephonic download. What interests me, again, is this Lovecraftian horror that slumbers just beyond view. And now you don't even need to locate a copy of the Necronomicon to access it. Just open a game file, pick up a phone. Where you've already screwed yourself just by being curious. Like 'I wonder what this Cthulhu is.' Famous last words.

Don't even go there. It was OK when he was asleep at the bottom of the ocean. Why did you have to go and get all excited by him? There's a number of different ways of thinking about that fantasy. But one of them surely has to do with the hyperobjects, right? One little tiny thing that you do, that is statistically meaningless, scales up to a gigantic action that is very destructive. So it's not even the actual act, just the flicker of curiosity that invites you to download. There's a *Dr. Who* episode I just watched where teenagers log on to a readily available Internet service that is of course a way for an alien to come and take control of them. Simply by clicking on that particular wireless option, you have promulgated its imminent arrival and destruction of all things good. Fascinating. Of course you could always look at these things as an extinction fantasy but when they're so popular with teenagers I have to feel that there's something else going on there. Have you seen *Interstellar* yet? No. Tell me more.

You should but you probably know the outlines of it already. An anthropocenic planet being devastated by plague, the last hope of humanity is to find another planet that they can depart to. Reading *Homestuck* against *Interstellar* was, for me, an aha moment. In a way, *Interstellar* actually feels like the more cartoonish response to the Anthropocene, apologetic, self-serious, weirdly predictable. *Homestuck* is a rebus universe where everyone involved is trying—and sometimes having fun trying—to figure out what the hell is going on. I have an interpretation! Interpretation imminent. Download, please.

What if it was the opposite of the official explanation for itself? In other words, what if the idea that you'd caused a calamity simply by looking at something or being curious or some poor little adolescent flicker of, you know, the 'I wonder what sex is all about...ahhh!' If I was a psychoanalyst, that's presumably where I'd go with it. What if that was precisely the fantasy that was blocking something much more mundane, yet worse, or more oppressive? In other words, what if the idea of that tiny flicker setting off this global fire was one of the last gasp ways that this Enlightenment anthropocentrism manifests itself? This is something that I've said sometimes about speculative realism. That it's sort of like the universe is a horror universe, but that horror is still my human reaction to it. But it's like the very limit of my human being's anthropocentrism. Finally I'm horrified by my reason, and my reason itself is horrifying, and instead of soaring into the heaven, I'm rubbernecking my inclusion in the Cthulhu-like multipodal abyss of horror.

And somehow that is a way of telling myself or horrifying myself into admitting to myself that there are nonhumans in my social space that I need to take care of. In other words, the mundane problem of 'maybe I should rewire my house so that it doesn't drain so much energy off the grid,' or 'maybe I should get a little solar power going for my street or my village or my town,' or 'maybe I should get together with a group of people and rewire the grid,' is what we're blocking here. We know it already but we're blocking it. I'm not speaking against the adolescents here and not saying that they've been conned. But maybe it has something to do with the teenager as a consumerist category that the commodity world is trying to excite into not caring for the nonhuman in the most mundane, boring, possible ways.

Not that they've been duped necessarily. But because the fantasy is about how my innocent little libido is caught inevitably in this process that I can't control, in the end this is precisely a fantasy about how this big thing is real. It is speculative realism because, like UKIP, I have to invent a big global force that is oppressing me in order to comfort myself. Strangely, it's quite comforting to imagine that I'm just a little sucker on the tentacle of Cthulhu. Rather than imagining that I'm an agent in a world of other agents, where we have this interminable task of getting along with one another that's actually much more irksome and irritating and draining of my little libido. If a tiny thing that I do brings this extremely negative orgasm of bliss-horror into my world—destructive, incandescent—I am actually inhibiting the ways in which I could imagine plugging my libido into energy networks, literally, that might superficially seem quite dull and familiar. You know, cathecting, 'let's put solar panels on the roof...' That's exactly right. One has to make a distinction between a functional state of hyposubjectivity—in other words, a baseline bare life hyposubjectivity that's constituted by the hyperobjects that we're coming to recognize and understand and fear and wonder about—and the potentiality of what could be done with one's hyposubjectivity once it is recognized and embraced as such.

There are latent forms and also more energized, self-aware ways of being a hyposubject. That's the critical thing with hyperobjects, too. The world changes once you know they're there, just like the world changes once you know you're on Cthulhu's tentacle. It's never the same again. The horror is in that reckoning. And madness follows. Madness being the punishment for voicing the things that have to remain unspoken for the contemporary world to exist as it does. And there your analysis is really good. You are pointing to how through the pursuit of bliss-horror, we deflect ourselves from investing in ideas and behaviors that would actually, at a mass level, make a difference. This is the functional type of hyposubjective experience, by which I mean "functional" in terms of maintaining the current anthropocenic trajectory of things. In terms of the planet and its species, it's actually highly dysfunctional.

It's double-edged, isn't it? You could get stuck there, is the point. My absurd D&D map of ecological practice starts with guilt. That the reason to act is that you've done something wrong. And then eventually you realize, the reason to act is because I am wrong. I become horrified by my own horrible stuff. Horror is one level below shame. It's more phenomenologically accurate and it's more compelling than the shame of being a human who doesn't even recycle or whose recycling efforts are haphazard. So it's realistic in that sense. But in another way, you could get stuck there.

And this is speaking to the hope of the teenager, that actually the horror is a necessary stage, and it's appropriate for teenagers to get into the horror and work through it. It's the adults that put the horror shows together and then make money off of publishing essays about them that I want to have a word with. It's the corporations that transact in all these horrible things. Because, in a way, the adolescent horror is a much less cynical horror. It's actually a necessary experience. Of course it's isomorphic with the necessary experience of being guilty, ashamed, and then being horrified by your emerging sexuality over which you also have no control. You know, there are these hormones, and I'm in this body. I am a sucker on a tentacle, actually. That's a necessary moment, but not a moment at which someone wants to get caught. Maybe a hyposubject's emergence does pass through a phase like that. But it's the people who want to get stuck there, who want to constantly peddle horror, those are the ones to watch out for. It's how we address this question of 'what do we do about our energy,' because we could write another book about how everything is totally fucked because of Big Oil. Or we could write a book like this one, which is what I hope we're doing, that we aren't totally fucked. That actually, it's perfectly possible to rejig the grid. Or as we said before, to occupy or squat the grid. And to disable it bit by bit from the inside.

With my ideology critique hat on, I can see how this horror image is a way of sustaining or feeling that there is a big picture despite my tiny pathetic meaningless human whatever whatever whatever. Which is like an upside down dystopian Enlightenment thought. But then, just to summarize, it's actually also a way station on a path to something quite different. A dialectical image, isn't it? It is. And this is why gaming is so important. To my mind, gaming is not only a place not for fantasy and experiment but also a place for the training of the imagination to work across scales and phases and locations. Gaming is how the hyposubject can learn and extend its abilities. Gaming is world-opening and that is important in our situation. Where the world as such interpellates us to go along with things as we are, whispers that we're path-dependent, that it's a rigged game, that any happy life depends on the services provided by oil companies and grids, that nothing will ever change, and so why not go ahead and make the best of it. But game ideation is a place where unexpected thoughtlines can begin to develop. Sure, gaming has social institutional structure, we all know that. But it's something to be taken seriously. Clearly, corporations are taking it seriously. The whole phenomenon of gameification: where not only must you work really hard and look like you're enjoying your work, but actually really enjoy it, for real.

Otherwise you won't be able to score points in this game, which is tantamount to actually doing your work because the work interface is now a game. So you have to allow the libido of the corporation to leech itself off of you, to penetrate you, to that extent. That suggests that games—we're talking about video games right—are potent beasts. Video, but also tabletop, also role-playing. There are a lot of different kinds of gaming, and all of them should be taken seriously in this process. When you think about what might enroll people in taking their hyposubjectivity seriously. An academic essay or a film certainly has some potential to do that. But when you think about technologies of the self that are widely available, and that attract people through their sheerly ludic qualities—even when they aren't actually sure of what it is they're attracted to—then you have to think about games. Strangely, during the late 1970s, in parallel with the rise of *Dungeons & Dragons*, there emerged *The Call of Cthulhu* role-playing game. I know that one, I've played it before. Tell me about it. Because in a way, it's quite counterintuitive that you'd be able to make a game out of it. Because presumably the whole idea is that this is the universe that we're in. You can't adjust it. But making it into a role-playing game at least suggests the possibility that different things could happen.

You and I are both of that generation, too, we both played *D&D*. In most of those games, you had your character sheets and you had your dice and you had your rulebooks. But what attracted me and my friends to *The Call of Cthulhu* was that it was very amenable to freer imaginative play, at least how we did it. We were already quite familiar with the Lovecraft universe. So it became more of an improvised performance, and the game master essentially operated as a storyteller, setting up a mystery that could be explored through the game play. The thing is, the beasts were so—Absurd. Absurd, but also deadly. Absurdly deadly.

They would drive you mad. And to be honest the formal game mechanics were not really up to the task of summoning Lovecraft's universe. Because if you followed the rules strictly you might have these moments like, 'roll a die to see if you're driven into gibbering madness.' Somehow that didn't quite capture for me the spirit of Lovecraft, which was, as we've been talking about it, this sense of living on the cusp of the monstrous, feeling the cold chill of impending recognition. And in that way, we felt it demanded something different than the kind *Dungeons & Dragons* adventures that we played, which was more a kind of mundane, wage laborious 'let's go down into the dungeon and do our eight hours,' come back out with our loot and go spend it. The Cthulhu mythos was about the possibility of encountering something of a radically different scale and significance that would leave you utterly transformed. In Benjamin's terms it was a matter of experiencing messianic time. Not just slogging through homogenous linear time. Not just building the past out over the future, like pouring concrete over what once was a forest.

Fascinatingly, the extremely control-freaky and pettifogging dungeon master—aren't they all?—who was our main guy, sent us off into a world in which it gradually dawned on everyone after several months of trying to figure out what the hell this different dimension was about that it was a dimension of the Cthulhu mythos. Slowly it emerged that the only real solution was to get the fuck out of it. Anyway, I know what you mean. Role playing games are quite interesting actually. I'm very keen on thinking about how aesthetic formats aren't necessarily restricted to the physical medium in which they finally reside. It's quite clear to me that Wordsworth invented cinema in a certain way. The way he writes poetry opens up a fantasy space in which something like making celluloid movies becomes important— these really long narratives where there's this shifting gaze and this intrinsic motile quality. Even when you look at his poetry, page after page of blank verse resembling inch after inch, foot after foot of celluloid movie film. So I wonder whether those role-playing games open up a fantasy space in which something like a video game about hyposubjects could be thought or thinkable. I think they do. And you're pointing out that one had to ignore the fundamental parameters of *The Call of Cthulhu* in order to inhabit that world in a way that made sense as a role-player. That does in fact seem really isometric with the political task that we have before us of needing to ignore what we take to be the horrifying totalized world of complete oil.

The *Cyclonopedia* world. Negarestani's naphthology. It's that world, the Cthulhu world, multiplied by oil or mediated through it. A brilliant project. Somehow the hyposubject weirdly becomes more politically effective when ignoring this dislocated totality. If you get caught in the headlights of it, you can't possibly act. You're paralyzed by a kind of cynical reason. Since everything you do in the game space eventually involves you going insane—because presumably the likelihood that you're going to go insane when you roll the dice becomes higher and higher the further you go. In *D&D* terms the Lovecraft monsters had -20 charisma, which basically meant that when you saw them, you would go completely round the bend. Do you remember the one called The Black She-Goat of the Woods with a Thousand Young?

Shub-Niggurath I think. Shub-Niggurath! What a name. Both misogynist and racist. Well, Lovecraft was both. Right? Score. As this project moves ahead, I think we should push hard on the idea that hyposubjectivity offers very fertile ground for game-making and gamer-making. That should be part of what we seek to do, to think exactly how you would render the hyposubject through gaming. Instead of *A Thousand Plateaus,* is it A Thousand Video Games? Or just A Thousand Games. Video games are amazing in many respects these days but they've still got a ways to go before they're going to be as good as role-playing games in terms of unfettering the imagination. For the moment, they're beautiful. Video games are going to replace cinema eventually.

They're gaining on cinema rapidly. And cinema will undergo a massive transformation in response to video gaming and its heightened interactivity, open worlds and greater influence over storylines and outcomes.

If what we are saying is valid, then the playful attitude towards the political is also a kind of game space. Political action also becomes a kind of role-play. Just like Jón Gnarr in the mayor's office in Reykjavík. I think he was engaged in a very serious game there. That was the whole idea, to bring LARPing into the political sphere. Role-play has some kind of affinity, or maybe more than affinity, with political action.

To circle back to where we started today, if we're living in a world where we're being asked to inhabit these dreary political fantasies and games—the games of the UKIPs and the games of the Tea Party and the other people who are being baited into taking part in those games—then why shouldn't we be calling for a proliferation of new kinds of speculative attachments and practices that could take those game media we already have available to us and work through them to unlock new political possibilities?

Simply to dismiss these phenomena as not only regressive, but the sort of 'we've been here before' types of neo-Fascism that should be immediately discounted, is not to notice that UKIP are basically

LARPers who would love it if they were the only game around. Because other political formations are not game-like at all. There is something that they've tapped into that has a grip on people. So we need more UKIPs, strangely. But different, antiracist antinationalist ones. The UKIP people still aspire to become hypersubjects in their own way.

The Best Party has this word "Best." UKIP has "Independence," you know, UK Independence. And the word "best" evokes that 'we're going to take the best of all the policies and smash them all together, no matter what those are.' Ideology be damned. It's an algorithm. That's the similarity. No matter what else I'm going to say, you know I'll end up saying that the UK must be independent of Europe. There's a rule to my political statements. For the Best Party, there's a rule too but it's just an ironic thumbs-up gesture. Which seems an infinite improvement.

IV subtraction, transcendence, excess, implosion, singularity, subscendence, unplugging, roombas

What kinds of beings can be hyposubjects? We've talked a lot about human beings, but what about other types of beings? Someone who is not sympathetic would say, "Oh, look at them being all anthropocentric even while trying to make an intervention in the Anthropocene. And one of them is an anthropologist." That's an awful lot of anthros in one sentence.

That's kind of where we're at. So perhaps this would be an apt moment to expand the conversation. Is the concept of hyposubject robust enough to include the nonhuman? Must it necessarily include the nonhuman? The word 'robust' is precisely right. What I like about the notion of hyposubjects is that it feels subtractive. You take away some features of the subject, thus allowing it to percolate into domains that we normally don't allow. It's not eliminative, but rather subtractive, if we can make that distinction. We're not saying that, 'we're all made of atoms and that's why we're equally valid.'

We're saying that there is something about the hypo- quality of the hyposubject that allows it to be exported into categorical domains that we normally don't associate with subjectivity. In a way, the concept is 'weak.' Not that it's invalid, but it's a very defanged concept of subject. Or perhaps it's just a feral concept. We don't want to overdomesticate, overrationalize it, because that's precisely not the point of the whole line of thought we've been pursuing here.

Apropos of domestication, I've just been on the radio talking about the dreaded concept of the singularity and this idea that humans once again can transcend themselves. This idea, at once horrific and utopian, that we're going to go through a period where artificial intelligence becomes more powerful than us, and we can use that to upload ourselves into the cloud, and all these things that Ray Kurzweil thinks are a good idea. Like the maniacal avoidance of death, which some psychoanalysts would say is precisely death itself. I think that's a classic human story—that we're capable of transcending ourselves—and I feel like the language of domestication and the language of self-transcending pair together a bit. At least, why is it that when we read somebody like Heidegger—and he's full of these very feudal agricultural motifs—is it that this idea of Dasein is the thing that transcends itself and that transcends its world all the time, and therefore allows other beings, graciously, to fall into its destinal, lawn-mowing path?

On the one hand, it would be nice to allow other kinds of beings to be able to do that—like sheep and grass. Then, on the other hand, maybe doing that isn't exactly what we're after with this concept of hyposubjects. Maybe the whole idea of hyposubjects is being that can't actually transcend itself.

Multispecies is part of the whole ecology of thinking today in a very important way. It aspires, persuasively I think, toward a project that really, finally, this-is-the-real-shit-now, seeks refuge from the empire of Northern Western privilege by questioning the pinnacle on which that kind of humanity made its Humanity, capital H. By beginning to think about relationships between species and the responsibilities we have to each other, the mutual kinds of enablement. Donna Haraway is so important and despite being very well-known, somehow still never gets the credit she actually deserves. For *Primate Visions* which set Latour on his way. But also for *Modest_Witness*, which is such a powerful statement of the massive marshaling of nonhuman labor that was necessary to create the floating world of Modernity that Humanity wants to live in. All of the testing, all of the experimentation, all of the muscle labor.

Add to that the photosynthesis that makes solar energy usable by all non-photosynthetic beings. There's nothing without the photosynthesizers. I'm very into the OncoMouse essay. One could argue that a kind of Western agricultural mode, which remains one of our big problems, is a kind of dispositif, a paraknowledge regime. It's an elephant in the room that sucks other beings into its orbit, and disposes of them quite literally. And it seems to me that the project is to think of a way to crawl out from under it rather than to transcend it, because transcendence is precisely the operational mode of agriculture. 'We're going to somehow transcend our material conditions.' 'We're going to be able to open a time horizon that's longer than our two or three-week subsistence temporality.' Odd, isn't it, that these kinds of subsistence temporalities coexist with a much more expansive dreamtime ontology—or is it a hauntology?—where time is vast and liquid and going everywhere.

And, not to go on and on about it, but this is precisely my problem with what the quite talented Christopher Nolan did in that film *Interstellar*. It's precisely all about transcendence. It's exactly the same as when you talk to people invested in the oil and gas industry here in Houston, who believe that we're one magical, technological breakthrough in carbon sequestration away from being able to pump as much oil as we want and still live in clean, sustainable environments and everything, or at least everything we care about, will be fine. It's a powerful and seductive fantasy.

The point being that even if that's true, this is a moment in which to think otherwise. Even if it's true that we could push a button and all our problems would go away ecologically, would we want to live in a world where the button-pushing is done by a massive oil corporation that is still coordinated with this epistemic dispositif? And of course the 'we' in the white oil man's sentence is 'we humans.' It takes no account of other species and so forth. So—sorry, this is a bit of a tangent—when you talk about the importance of the agricultural revolution, of agrilogistics, is it precisely about the ordering of other forms of life to serve the human? Is that the issue you are bringing into focus? We develop the perennial planting of corn to make it durably productive for human life and so that we can stay in one place. Thus everything else becomes organized as food and labor for us.

In a certain way, everything is doing that all the time; we're always arranging things according to our concepts of them. And maybe bits of lettuce arrange themselves on forks according to their concept of forks. I don't know, I'm not a bit of lettuce. But in a way, everything is shaping the world to its own ends in a certain way. It's just that the implicit philosophy behind the agrilogistics is, when scaled up to earth magnitude and left to run for 12,000 years, obviously toxic to other life forms. And one of the things it does is establish a thin rigid boundary between what is inside and outside social space, being categorized as human plus cattle. And etymologically of course, fascinatingly, cattle, capital, chattle—they're actually all the same. I didn't quite realize that until last week, that cattle and capital are the same. I've just been reading Sloterdijk and one of the things he says is that thinking energy is one scale higher than thinking human economic relations. And that there is a new proletariat, namely cows.

He's saying that these beings should be seen as a new kind of proletariat. They're being produced and farmed and slaughtered on an unbelievable scale. The difference between what we've been doing in the last twenty or thirty years, and what we've done, period, is quite extraordinary. But it's kind of a wash-rinse-repeat of the philosophy that things are manipulable lumps decorated with accidents. And that existing is better than any quality of not existing. So it's better to have big juicy grains of wheat than tiny small grains of wheat and pretty flowers, you see. It's a war against what we take to be meaningless appearance. So one thing we don't want to do when we talk about hyposubjects is to say, underneath, worms and dolphins and humans are basically the same kind of lump. We should not be reductionists in that way. We might want instead to define what the opposite of masterful transcending would be, if it isn't simply being a component in a machine that you can't possibly change. I like that move.

Could one say that instead of transcending you could develop a greater susceptibility? That's one thing I keep thinking about. That maybe the opposite would be becoming more susceptible to a larger variety of things that aren't you, most of which are nonhuman—including your own body to a certain extent. To that extent, the human species is not human in a certain way. Reminding ourselves of our gut bacteria and other microbes, microorganisms in our bodies that outnumber our human cells 10 to 1. They're small but they're agentive. I think what you're saying is that we need to pay attention to the fact that we are susceptible and interconnected with other beings. And that in the Anthropocene with its looming hyperobjects that we experience new kinds of susceptibilities, but also discover new potential alliances. For example, between the cattle who die in genocidal industrial slaughterhouses and the humans whose homes are being overcome by rising seawater and who are being driven to become refugees. Both are forms of life that are being extinguished by interrelated processes, and they have common interests that are rarely identified as such.

So there's interrelationship and susceptibility. And then, at a more political level, there are alliances. Realizing that you can't do without your gut bacteria, you could become susceptible, phenomenologically, to them, which would then erode your sense of specialness and mastery. That would then encourage you to form an alliance—that is the political movement we are sensing.

It also requires recognition. I mean that in Haraway's sense that we need to recognize and recover the enormous quantity of nonhuman and human labor that was required to constitute Modernity. That labor has been completely silenced and occluded behind institutional walls. Unseen, unthought. We only hear about human invention and genius and breakthroughs. And this is all about transcendence again. We never hear about all the life that was orchestrated to make it happen.

And when we hear about the great geniuses that invent things, we never even hear about their huge teams of support staff. I don't think any one physicist could possibly be in charge of CERN anymore, if at all, ever. It's this tendency toward copyright control, based on some notion of private property, and it devolves into treating most other beings as the abject invisible cattle that exist simply to make the idea emerge. But we can't allow it to become an ontological reduction to a general category of life, a One that unites us all. That smuggles transcendence in again. It's a prime biopolitical category, isn't it? If we're all the same underneath, then it's even easier to manipulate us.

And why shouldn't humans lead things? Because we're so obviously the smartest class of beings there is, the most powerful, the chosen.

So this idea that we have solidarity because we're all alive, it might be the worst kind of pseudo-alliance that we could possibly have. It's not an alliance is it? Because an alliance is necessarily finite. This idea, this appeal to a complete universal umbrella—life—is precisely the problem. I was thinking about this in terms of rights the other day, and this is not to say that we shouldn't try to campaign for chimpanzees to have the right to leave the zoo, as some people are. But rather it is to say that if you apply rights in a generous, benevolent, anthropocentric way to all life forms whatsoever, they cease to have meaning. Rights depend upon exclusion, because rights depend upon the notion of possession and property, and moreover, private property.

So so you end up with paradoxical ideas such as the AIDS virus has just as much a right as this guy who's got AIDS to exist. So the model of interspecies alliance in the name of life breaks down quickly. You have to view the alliances as necessarily fragile, transitory and at times violent. If you've decided that you don't want the AIDS virus, you're going to team up with some AZT. You're going to want AZT as an actor in your network if you want to be Latourian about it. That's a good point. There is a rosy vision in which all the small creatures of the world can bond together because of their common interests and overcome the hyperobjects and hypersubjects. It appeals to me politically but it's not sufficient analytically.

Or maybe instead of thinking of ourselves as everything, we could think of ourselves as an enormous something that isn't everything. In a way, it's Feuerbach's idea of species that gets translated into Marx's idea of species-being. In refuting theism, Feuerbach argues that all the qualities we attribute to god are qualities of us that we've alienated. So, god is love means love is god, as John Lennon said. And species is not a universal category because in fact it's a highly specific, yet very large, yet still thinkable entity that we comprise. There's a weird way in which he's not saying we are really little tiny people without god and without hope. He's actually saying, potentially we're super beings. We have this superpower of being a collective that has a specific color and flavor to it; we're humans.

That resonates with Nietzsche, too. Eric Santner makes a wonderful point about the Nietzschean übermensch that if you think about what über means in German, it's not 'over;' so 'overman' is the wrong translation. Über is more like a volcano whose lava is spilling outside of its crater. It's a condition of excess so übermensch is the excessively human, the 'excessman'. It's the being that's always already spilling outside of itself. There one also senses the deeper crypto-Hegelian trope of constant dialectical process in which becoming is always overwhelming being, always confronting it, negating it, leaving being in its wake as it moves on to something else. Now whether that something else is always a more perfect, sublime form, I'm not sure.

Like Malcolm Bull, I feel that attempts to overcome Nietzsche—the clue is in the phrase—end up falling back into Nietzsche. But what about implosion? So that instead of bubbling out of myself, I'm collapsing into more things than myself. There's an excess, but it's not something that's bursting out, but rather something that's imploding me—like my gut bacteria could easily do. So what we're talking about is not a kind of force with no reverse gear. We're trying to think of a way to rethink what something like transcendence would mean without the idea of increasing mastery and its cognate words like history, destiny, spirit.

Because mastery, transcendence, excess—that is the world that we know. Those are the qualities of this era. And with the refinement of excessive mastery in various localities has emerged relentless predatory impulses — monotheistic, capitalistic — to bring the world into alignment with our transcendence mission. An imploded form of subjectivity is worth considering as an antidote. One that is denser, but also more aware of the architecture of its density and of the gravitational forces that hold it together, one that is not constantly seeking the beyond.

Think about butoh, the Japanese dance of death that arose after Hiroshima. It explores an aesthetics of allowing your body to implode, allowing gravity to pull you towards earth, rather than trying to soar beyond gravity, or move despite gravity. You allow yourself to be sucked down. So perhaps the model is not the volcano, it's more like the bubbling geothermal mud, if you want to think of it Iceland style, bubbles that collapse. I'm also very interested right now in the trope of invagination. Don't get me started on it, but it's this idea of turning things inside out, that I think is complicit in the idea of implosion. It's something that happens in chiasmus that usually gets repressed. You know, when Kennedy says, "ask not what your country can do for you, but what you can do for your country," he's trying to say that what you can do for your country is better, more attuned to the real because we're all individual Americans. But what actually happens is that one term implodes into the other, and at the middle of that x, which is the chiasmus, there's a moment of fundamental ambiguity. And this moment is achieved through this sucking inward called invagination. Chiasmus is a way that power likes to bamboozle people. But clearly it's also something unfriendly to power. Which might precisely be why power uses it, to defang it in advance. So again, if it's not leaping over oneself, but allowing oneself to implode, I think invagination—at least in rhetorical terms—that's the action that's happening.

All this terrain was mapped by feminist philosophers in the early 70s. What they say about women could be applied to other life forms. It's a potential pathway to thinking 'what would it be if we weren't beings who established our destiny.' What if that wasn't what being an entity consisted of. It would have to be thinkable along the lines, articulated in there. The notion of a multiplicity of physical qualities that can't be reduced to, in the feminist discourse, a phallus or the penis. We're not talking about one organ, we're talking about many many organs. It's not 'body without organs', it's something else.

Some humans now have the aspiration to know what lettuce is thinking, which I think is part of the same dispositif, the desire to inhabit other life subjectivities in the name of empathy or understanding. Those humans aren't typically the mass of carnivores going about their daily business of course but rather those who advocate we imagine what it's like to be the cow in the slaughterhouse, feeling the cow's terror. I support the politics of these interventions. But what I'm never certain about is where the impulse of dyslocating human subjectivity leaves off and where the impulse of occupying, colonizing even, non-human subjectivity begins. I think we need to be alert to the presence of the cunning of predator reason even within projects of implosion, dyslocation, multispecies alliance building.

There are now machines that can tell you what you're dreaming. They map your brain firings in a pixelated 3D space, and correlate those 3D pixels to an infinite supply of YouTube videos that suggest the movements and things about which you're dreaming. It's uncanny how accurate it is. In a way, a machine that can tell you what your brain is coming up with might be similar to being able to know what it's like to be a lettuce leaf. It scares me actually, I had a reaction to wanting that.

Would it work even with the absence of a central nervous system and specialized neural cells? I wonder. That seems like a model that might act to visualize the consciousness for some kinds of beings but for others. Also it's obviously a symptom of the incredibly sadistic voyeurism, the endless putting out of images, that's part of our current condition. You know how, on Facebook, pictures of one's nearest and dearest are in fact inhibiting people from really seeing them in a certain way. Aristotle was quite right to say that the murder that should happen offstage, not because it's taboo, but because when you put it on stage, it's always less than what you might think when you can't see it. So there's something about attunement to what it might be like to be a lettuce leaf that might not have to do with sadistically being able to see all of it and being able to tweet—live tweet—every possible modality of it. But the fact that we can actually ask such a question in the academy now with some sense of humor but without a sense of absolute nonsense is an interesting moment. But of course, who am I? I'm not a piece of lettuce. But I probably can't tell you very much about what it's like to be me. Personhood is an intersubjective property. You pass my Turing test to get it. To the extent that I'm paranoid that you may not be a person, you are a person. And so somehow, the personhood of the lettuce leaf is an intersubjective fact that is necessarily, at this point, a politicized debate. A debate that has only just begun.

One wonders how human beings came to recognize each other as persons in the first place. Often they didn't and still don't obviously. But where they did presumably there was a politics of decision that has been forgotten, ignored, blanked out, as we've gone further into treating each other like people. To return to an earlier theme, hyposubjects necessarily include nonhumans, because hyposubjectivity always has more in it than it itself. The whole is always less than the sum of its parts. That was one of our original slogans. It's like Houston, a place that is very difficult to understand. Houston, as megacity, is much less than the totality of all the houses and streets and pathways and insane routes through insane sprawl that Houston is. Yet we keep looking for some greater whole. Ironically, despite being home to a large population of hypersubjects, the city itself is profoundly hyposubjective, it is constantly squatting inside of itself.

I was talking about this in an architecture class a couple weeks ago. People want to see the megacity from above and beyond, in a way that transcends the streets. But the thing about a megacity is that it doesn't transcend its streets. That's what makes it different from a London or a Paris. The megacity shows you something, which is that the whole is always less than the sum of its parts. It's an intuitive paradox when one lives in Houston.

Here's another issue: whether the emphasis on knowledge, inevitably involves a new project of mastery and transcendence through incorporation, so that knowing how the lettuce feels is to have assimilated it, in a Borg-like way, into the collective. Mastery and transcendence are always there whispering to us that our next knowledge project, our next project of understanding, will be our redemption. We're very good at it. We've practiced it in many different modes for at least 12,500 years. It's been a long deep programming process. I've just been talking about singularities, where the singularity advocates are all very excited that a huge change will happen in about a decade or so. I'm therefore very wary about the idea we can get over ourselves or under ourselves in the next ten years. Why ten years? What do they think will happen in the next ten years?

There's a business model that combines Moore's law and the accelerating value of information technology to produce a logarithmic curve, and the curve begins to go almost vertical in 2020—somewhere between 2020 and 2040. Which means, according to Ray Kurzweil, that something the size of a blood cell will have an iPhone's computing power. And thus you could have iPhone computing power all throughout your body. Which means that you'll become so much wiser and billions of time more intelligent than you are now. Define 'intelligence' please, Mr. Kurzweil. Define 'billions of times greater than,' and 'wiser.' He says that one of the things we will do is resist death, and upload ourselves to the cloud, whatever that means. The fact that this is going to involve an awful lot of rare Earth elements— And electricity!

And electricity. And thus we will come to achieve what some Silicon Valley guy thinks is transcending human being. It's definitely a guy's way of thinking rather than a gal's. And it's therefore no surprise that these male computer engineers are all very excited about it. It's basically Christian millennial apocalypticism without the inconvenience of sin and redemption. So that you can go through an apocalypse and come out transfigured. Living forever. Beyond even a cyborg. Pure consciousness enabled by an immortal machine-body. Perfect reason, perfect power.

And a perfect relationship between you, the transhumanist self-transcending human, and the artificial intelligence that you now realize totally outstrips you. To me this is actually the case. We're surrounded by things that are much more clever than us, just by dint of being a part of a biosphere. It's already the case that we can't walk across a street without being immersed in thousands of systems that are, in a way, smarter than we are—I mean, look at the gut bacteria again. This whole techno-fantasy is really about transcending the physical in the final analysis. What's scary about artificial intelligence being smarter than you is what's scary about women being more powerful than you. I suspect the whole singularity fantasy is a displaced reaction to feminism.

And mortality and reproduction and children and perhaps also the Anthropocene. The desire is that the white male should be able to live forever, think forever, in perfect singularity. Even if—and this is the interesting thing—it ends up being the case that white masculinity is just software loaded onto a machine. Somehow that virtual 'life' seems preferable to living as wetware in a world where the dominion of white men has been compromised. Another movie, again not a very good one, that comes to mind is the Johnny Depp movie, *Transcendence*, where Depp, the brilliant scientist facing mortal collapse, is uploaded into the web. Not only does he survive there but he actually thrives. With all the data in the web now at his disposal, his consciousness achieves still greater levels of insight, makes still greater technological breakthroughs. He achieves a near perfect state of mastery over materials, beings, environments. It's helpful that the movie isn't very nuanced in terms of plot and characterization because the fantasy oozes everywhere, painted in bright red letters. I can imagine the pitch in Hollywood, 'suppose you could become more than human and live forever in the web.' I'm sure that very much appealed to all those white male film industry decision makers staring down their own mortality and looking to Silicon Valley for salvation.

So here's the politics of something we might call subscendence as opposed to transcendence. Trans- usually signals overcoming, going beyond. But sub- is about being close to, beneath, within, less than. The transcendence narrative has to do with inhabiting some grid-like structure that's much bigger than me, in a much better way, that enables me to be much more powerful. So maybe the first move is to see something like *The Matrix* as an energy system rather than as a service provider of virtual reality. The important thing being not so much the content conveyed, but rather the energetic infrastructure itself. And then, instead of seeking to transcend my physicality, I try to subscend my fantasy of disembodiment and its perfect marriage in heaven between the misogynistically disembodied matrix and my own inevitably white male power trip. That becomes an identification with the poor nonhuman beings, such as one's own flesh, that have gone to the trouble of allowing you to think fantasies of yourself. I think "subscendence" is beautiful by the way. "Hyposubjects subscend" is another slogan to play with.

Subscendence and unplugging from the grid. It speaks to the need for energy humanities, because as Sloterdijk's pointed out, whether or not it's a Soviet or capitalist situation, if it's powered by massive energy grids, in the form of carbon-powered electricity, it remains the essence of the problem. There's a funny moment at the end of *The Matrix* where Neo plugs himself in to the energy system and completes some kind of circuit that allows everyone to have a much nicer time in the Matrix. I can't help but think that's a sort of circle-squaring, Vitruvian man, sweet spot fantasy in which we have transcendence of the human without catastrophe. The singularity folks talk as though transcendence is going to be really benign. This is not going to be a *Terminator* scenario. This is going to make us so much wiser and better and smarter. And then, we'll be able to look after the animals. But it's like, when's that then? As if to say, once we white guys get our shit worked out, then we'll be able to help out everyone else.

So along with transcendence, there's a deferral of the political. Literally. I'm going to wait until I'm as great as I can possibly be before I figure out what to do. Which will probably have something to do with going to Mars, in some virtual form, and then downloading myself into something Martian. Whereas the hyposubjective counterpart to this strategy of delaying action until transcendence is beginning things too quickly without a fully understood aim and a proper plan, and just trying to fumble through. I think hyposubjects are prepared to make a lot of mistakes.

Yes, they make a lot of mistakes. They're not afraid to be fools. Their political projects aren't orchestrated, transparent, forced movements, but rather implosive, deliquescent, projects of unplugging. If we take subscendence as a museword, then what do subscendent politics look like? What does a subscendent life look like? What is it to be less than the sum of your parts? I feel as though this whole process of trying to figure out a few things to say about hyposubjects has been training ourselves to subscend. Oh very much so. It's been a kind of wandering, testing things out. Diagnostics. But in a highly unscientific way. A fumbling diagnostics of the contemporary. Trying to figure out what it is that we are now. We're basically Roombas.

Roombas? Roombas of the philosophical. Actually that's quite perfect. It's the ultimate hyposubject isn't it? The Roomba is the perfect inverse to the Skynet/Matrix, transcendent hyperobject. A Roomba is always struggling to come into its agency. It probably feels quite imploded, it's got very limited programming. It knows it wants to get dirt inside of itself, everything else it has to figure out as it goes along, with a fairly limited sensory apparatus. So it sort of trundles along, bumping into walls and furniture, staying very close to the earth. Always less than itself.

It's basically a ZhuZhu pet that happens to clean things and that cats like to ride on. Do they? So the cats recognize Roombas as fellow hyposubjects, creatures to play and explore with? Yes, there's a whole genre of YouTube videos of cats sitting on Roombas, going around and around the house.

V subscendence, holism, dismantle the apocalypse, systems, androleukocene, desire, obesity, correlationism, smooth functioning, mental labor, scavengers

I wanted to announce that sometimes I can totally break subscendence down. Can you? Well then, that seems like a promising place to start. So, holism says that the whole is always greater than the sum of its parts, but this ontology we are discussing is actually claiming that the whole is less than the sum of its parts, which is why things that emerge from other things are very hard to locate, because we keep looking in the wrong direction. Basically you have to accept that sets can contain infinite numbers of things—which some people don't—and that sets can contain all kinds of contradictory, discrete things.

A set of things is one thing, but the things that it comprises are potentially an infinite regress. For example, highways are made up of concrete blocks that are just as real and important as the highway; those blocks are in turn made up of all sorts and sizes of aggregates that are just as real and important as the blocks. And so on and on. We then have a set that actually has more in it than the set itself as a concept. The insight is that a given concept set is actually ontologically smaller than the things it's drawing a line around. This gets us to a confrontation with neoliberalism where we can say: we can do it, we can do something else. Because we're beginning to understand that neoliberalism is actually something smaller than its components. Physically it might be huge; it covers the whole Earth with armed police officers. But, ontologically speaking, neoliberalism is smaller than one single polar bear.

One way in which ideology has trapped us into the cynical reason of thinking "there's no way to deal with this!" is through our habituation to a kind of default holism, which has a long history of dispositifs such as monotheism, where God is always bigger than you physically and ontologically. To that extent, the horrorcraft of speculative realism that says we're all part of Cthulhu's head is on the wrong side of the political spectrum. What we really need to do instead is to figure out that neoliberalism, global warming, and all these things are actually ontologically smaller and weaker than we suppose they are. Their components, including us, might easily overwhelm them ontologically.

Ideologies of holism and naturalism ask us to accept thingness on empirical grounds—this is a thing, a whole thing, because I can pick it up and manipulate it in a certain way—and then, with a sleight of hand, extend that thingness to invisible or imaginary wholes like Gods and Old Ones. But the cruelest trick of all may be that the very critical categories we might wish to deploy to draw attention to the sources of our hyperobjective condition—like "capitalism" or "global warming—also participate in that greater-than-the-sum-of-its-parts ontology. More holisms disabling us! As if they transcend, but what they really do is subscend. Subscendence happens when a set of things begins to exit its concept and becomes its own entities. When a set of things emerges as downwardly causal on its components then there is subscendence. And I heard from a Catholic theologian that it is in fact a term in theology! Amazingly and rather wonderfully, in some theology, Jesus subscends God. Someone has to.

Precisely because Jesus is physically embodied, finite, and weak. It resonates with ways in which people have been trying to rethink religion through radical politics recently. So, strangely enough, subscendence actually turns out to be a very handy concept right now. It was almost just a joke at first, but like many jokes its truth value subscends its silliness. What we've been talking about in this entire project has been more or less an arts of subscendent being. Subscendence is the point of departure because we're writing some kind of toolkit for how to change, how to unplug. For example, the energy grid subscends the uses and components of that energy grid. So it's perfectly possible for a small German town to switch off its part of the energy grid locally and become something else. It's absolutely simple and possible and doable. You turn a spigot off here, and then you turn a spigot off there. And then you start to create.

Because, if I understand this correctly, ontologically speaking a grid is composed of an almost infinite number of elements. It looks like a very big and impressive piece of transcendent machinery. But it is only that kind of machine to the extent that an enormous amount of labor is marshaled to constantly make it transcend. Its elements would tend on their own to subscend their participation in the project of gridness. A grid or a pipeline is then really nothing more than a mirage, an optical illusion of thingness produced by a certain project. Which is perhaps why across the world people are constantly tapping into grids and pipelines illegally and tinkering with them in all sorts of ways. It proves they are susceptible to transformation; we just need to intensify that susceptibility and to encourage more tinkering.

Yes, and this isn't reductionism. People will get angry if they think you are saying "reduced to" and they respond, "oh, you're saying that there are only individuals and no society?" We're not saying that. We're saying there is society, and it's physically very big actually, but it subscends; it's ontologically smaller than its members. I like this line of thinking. It's empowering somehow. And even if you don't go the set theory route, it still makes intuitive sense. It works philosophically but also phenomenologically at the same time. Absolutely. It's like I have this obsession with proving it logically somehow, but there's no really need to. Subscendence gives an edge to the notion of weakness people like Vattimo talk about. It literalizes it.

I was speaking in an architecture class about megacities the other day and I said, "You've just been looking for megacities in the wrong place, which is why you can't find them. You run into this problem of describing them." Just as we were saying before that all megacities, especially Houston, are less than the sum of the their parts. And of course all cities subscend. Thebes subscends. It's just really obvious with megacities, because they're so inflated, so amped up by globalization and neoliberalization and all of that. It's a helpful critical tactic too. Neoliberalism is always described as a global monolithic system that hoovers people and resources and ideas into itself. Like a black hole warping time and space.

But if we say that neoliberalism is actually much less than what it appears to be, that its elements can be commandeered or commandeer themselves in subscendent actions, then all of sudden the situation appears much less bleak. Because every small action of unplugging starts to matter so much more.

The way the dominant line of reasoning works today is that it says that neoliberalism (or whatever) is always one step ahead of you, it's always going to outthink what you do, and it's always going to co-opt what you do. But what if ontologically it was like a T-Rex, a really big and scary creature but with a tiny brain and tiny little arms that can easily topple over and become extinct. Such that it's true that our T-Rexes are powerful, and it's true that they are big, and it's true that we are suffering. But the way in which that truth is told sometimes is also a lie, a lie in the form of the truth. Because we absolutely can be and do something different; it's possible. It doesn't have to be like this, even if this, in the big picture, is a 12,000-year-old project. That's a long time but it's also not eternity, you see. Changing it could be almost ridiculously easy. The United Nations released something this summer that asked, "what if we shifted to small organic farms?" That would solve a lot of the emissions problem, and then another group is researching how if you devoted just ten percent of your farmland to indigenous species, you would help a great deal with the problems of energy throughput and species loss and pollution and the use of pesticides. Thinking that way acknowledges that the system you are trying to change is very big—look at the giant farms in Iowa!—but when you subscend ten percent of their fields and allow the little creepy crawlies to do their work, that "system" begins to look like something rather different. The point is we don't have to have an apocalyptic solution to an apocalyptic problem. We can dismantle the apocalypse.

"Dismantle the apocalypse" should be another slogan for hyposubjects. One of the limits we are facing is that our inherited critical practice often wishes to offer a hyperobjective solution to a hyperobjective problem. That's very well put. Once upon a time what was going to save us was the proletariat. But the proletariat is a hyperobject if I've ever heard of one. It's the imagined holistic antidote to the generalization of bourgeois society on a global basis. To be fair one of the things I always enjoyed about Marx's writing is he never used the word "capitalism." Not once. I don't think he saw the society he opposed as being ontologically systemic or even whole. It was always about capital for him, which was the formalization, but diverse formalization, of productive activity.

So however alienating and oppressive capital and capitalists might be, they were always entirely susceptible to the negation of the particular productive activity that brought them into being. Thus capital always contained within itself a transformative potential. So even if you want to believe that something like "capitalism" exists, it would be subscendent as well, with its own elements constantly generating friction and the basis for for capital's negation. So perhaps we need to return to the 19th century here to find our critical angle on the 21st century. In the 20th century meanwhile, from the 1930s onwards there's such a strong influence of cybernetic and other electronic modes of thinking. The systems theorists, the cyberneticians, social theorists like Luhmann (whom I find odious). The proposition of autopoietic systematicity is again the same holistic ontology in a different costume. You want to say to them: check your ontology please! Systematicity is a wholly death-driven and transcendent fantasy, which is the kind of ontology this planet can no longer afford.

It also reinforces a kind of paranoia that isn't helpful. Systems of what? Just as people forget that there are workers—because somehow it's a more satisfying or gratifying intellectual exercise to solve the Rubik's Cube without the soil and the worker. Remember the last sentence of Chapter 15 of *Capital*, Volume I—["Capitalist production, therefore, develops technology, and the combining together of various processes into a social whole, only by sapping the original sources of all wealth — the soil and the laborer"]— when you reinclude the soil and the worker in your estimation of capital, it's more like thinking about an algorithm. You have these materials to do this thing and then you pay people just a little bit less for more work or ask a little bit more work for the same amount of money and that's how you turn M into M', right? It's an algorithmic procedure. But you can also imagine a different procedure that doesn't sap the soil and the worker in the same way and which would thus cause the first algorithm to die on the vine. There's no need for this bleak sense that we're all part of a system. I mean "system" here also in the pre-systems theory sense. In the eighteenth and nineteenth centuries, it could also be used pejoratively to define an overarching, semi-invisible whole. I've noticed that certain shades of animal studies take the approach, "everything's going to be co-opted in advance; all of our resistance is futile, and yet we're going to resist anyway." Like the foundational gesture of Occupy where everybody is standing outside this huge bank with placards, yelling to no effect and someone says let's just go over to Zuccotti Park and take it over. Not that Occupy was the perfect whatever. But at least it was a serious and spontaneous effort to organize a different economy, which I take to mean a different way of organizing enjoyment. It was definitely an intervention into the grid, an unplugging.

Even if it was a weak intervention that seemingly "didn't accomplish anything." But its weakness was precisely its accomplishment. Just as we were saying that Jón [Gnarr]'s integration of vulnerability into the core of his political practice was one of his most important achievements. His embrace of ignorance—not ignorance in the absolute sense, that's what his critics, the proper politicians and media accused him of—but rather his embrace of the partiality of his understanding any number of things. That's what allowed him to ask for help, to encourage more people to engage in the process of understanding social problems and developing solutions to them. He likes to describe himself as the big spectacular buffoon who would attract all the attention and flak from the political establishment while all the while, under the radar, all these other very brilliant people would be able to do what needed to be done, unimpeded.

And he often was doing that while being fuzzed out with crushing headaches. He might be up on stage and forget the name of who was interviewing him and he would have to text Jóga to say, "I'm in trouble. Help me out." He was performing a broken leader, not a perfect leader. He allowed himself to be broken while also exuding charisma at the same time. It's like in his play, *Hotel Volkswagen*, which was actually better than his beloved Samuel Beckett. Jón's play was more generous, inclusive silliness. It subscends the mechanical absurdity of

Beckett. You might say that Beckett transcends. But Jón's play subscends Beckett.

I agree with you there. And while we are talking about Jón, a very
friendly and impressive person, but also another white guy, I think we
might pause a moment and interrogate our position as two white guys
who might appear to be trying to save the world. This is something
that will not be lost on others. Because after all it is white guys, more
or less, who brought us the Anthropocene, which is also very much the
Andropocene, the Leukocene and the Heterocene too. Neoliberalism,
that hyperobject we've been chewing over is also, to be very frank, an
economy of desire organized at a global scale to benefit not all people,
but specifically people like us. So it's not that one shouldn't try to
save the world. But the heroic savior position is another transcendental holist trick, isn't it?

And if I were another sort of person I would be troubled maybe
even to the point of paranoia about hypersubjects adopting the language of hyposubjects as an philosophical escape pod for precisely
the conditions they have been causing for some centuries or millen-
nia. I really do want to believe in a subscendent capacity for muta-
tion or reform. And maybe in that respect this project is designed to
sort of get under the skin of other hypersubjects. But I also think it's
incredibly important for the same reason that the project becomes
open source, expands beyond us, escapes us, somehow. At best I
can say that I aspire to hyposubjectivity but if I were a hyposubject I
would remain very suspicious of me, and rightly so. Clearly, the two
of us shouldn't be speaking for any 'them' in a holistic sense. When
Cymene and I were doing field research in a highly Indigenous region
of southern Mexico, working with people sometimes less than half
my size, the sheer physiology of hypersubjectivity struck me, how
much the scale of my current physical form has been the product of a
colonial-imperial regime centuries in the making. So if we're thinking about subjectivity also as an embodied condition, with historicity
written into our skeletal structures, then it's not as easy as snapping
one's fingers and saying 'let's go hypo!'

So true. I've seen pictures of mining families from the early 1920s
from England, and they are very short. Terry Eagleton, my tutor at
Oxford, is a good foot or two shorter than most of the upper-class
people there. It was something I noticed about Americans in the
1980s, that they were significantly taller and more robust somehow.
Although meanwhile the Brits have caught up. When I was more
deeply invested in the psychoanalytic theory, reading a lot of Freud
and Lacan and Zizek, I was convinced by their conceptualization of
endless unsatisfiable symptom-spewing desire as the fundamental

driver of the human psyche. But with a bit more distance and reflection that conviction of a psychic life driven by universal condition of desire is sounding awfully masculine doesn't it? And, beyond that, a product of western, elite, well-nourished masculinity. It's the view of psychic life from inside a particular economy that is designed to fulfill a particular kind of person's every desire. So, yes, desire becomes a constant state of suspension, for some.

I don't disagree but would slightly add or tweak, because recently I was at a conference called "Emergence" about atmosphere and architecture and design and there was a question in the Q&A where someone said, "Talk about obesity." And for half a second I didn't know what to say— because I usually give anyone the benefit of the doubt and I've never had such a question before. What everyone told me afterwards is that the question was inviting me to say something mean about fat people or why gluten is good or something like that. But I sort of improvised an answer, that I'll try to recreate in light of what you are saying, which I agree with but in a different modality.

Desire qua—this is the nub of the problem—desire qua—I want in the infinity. Why? Because I can do anything to anything. Lacan's formula for desire is the pursuit of the *objet petit a*. That means correlationism. The "a," superficially it's a Coke bottle, but it's actually my dream of myself as a cool kid, drinking a Coke, and I am constituted in relation to this thing. And that shakes down to a default, medieval, Aristotelian substance ontology, which is the smoking gun. Blank lumps, preformatted lumps, decorated with accidents later, as Lacan himself argues: I can do anything because everything is manipulable plastic. The trouble, of course, is that formula of Lacan's, which is the psychoanalytic formulization of consumerism, also contains within it a kind of sadism. Very much agreed. As though to say, "The real is just an effect of discourse and whatever I do, so I'm not really doing it to this person that I'm torturing." So then, the real qua women's sex organs, just to be provocative, always emerges as monstrous and frightening.

This kind of boy-horror starts to happen as the flip side to the boy-I-can-do-anything-to-anything, right? There's a weird, inverted dick measuring contest that starts to happen when people say, "My freaked out reaction to the real is much bigger than yours!" But is horror, or even anxiety, is it the top level? Is it the one emotion that never lies? Lacan forgot the other half of the formula, which I think could be supplied by someone like Irigaray or Object Oriented Ontology, which is that objet petit a desire is sitting on top of something else that we could call—if Lacan hadn't stolen all the letters—we could call it "O" for "Object." And it's only possible because there is a Coke bottle.

It's only possible, because this Coke bottle actually exceeds what I think of it, what I can do with it, how I use it in my world. It even exceeds itself somehow. This is what Irigaray says about genitality, that the body isn't just one thing reducible to another thing. It is, in fact, multiply equipped with a subscended multiplicity, as it were, of other kinds of bristling things that are and aren't it, so that woman is not one and not two.

Considering desire in this model one would say that the fantasy that I can do anything to anything is predicated on my always already being caught in a force field between me and at least one other entity that's already doing something to me. The Coke bottle is hailing me. The flip side is that Neanderthals would have loved Coca-Cola Zero, right? They would totally dig it. In a way, obesity for me is a kind of polymerase chain reaction blowup of something that's latent in not even human being, but in the way objects try to possess other objects. There's a chemical in consumerism, in other words, that might be useful for an ecological society. But we keep on trying to delete the whole thing, because, quite rightly as you say, the historical conditions are such, and consumerism right now is as you say it is, and it's definitely subtended by really aggressive, sadistic fantasies coming from some kind of correlationist version of Aristotle. In the future, when we've subscended the power grid, we might well not have as much food, which may make us quite upset in a way that people were upset before they started agriculture. Subscendence doesn't necessarily mean that we want less food. In other words, pathologizing obese people is a symptom of the kind of dispositif that we're talking about. It's like another kind of magic bullet solution, like if we could just get rid of obesity.

If we could just get rid of gluten! If we could take that out, the whole system would function smoothly. Smooth functioning is itself a concept. And we keep on wanting smooth functioning to function smoothly. We want this idea that problems can be patched over. Even a lot of environmentalism seems to be saying: if we just fixed this one little thing, then we'll be okay. In the end that would create a society so technocratic that I myself would rather live in outer space at that point. Ecological politics shouldn't be about trying to make things function smoothly. This is a long, convoluted answer to this question concerning desire, because histories of consumerism, Marx included, tend to talk about a period of smooth functioning that was then interrupted. The smooth functioning period is called "need." At some point we knew what we want, and we wanted what we knew. And there was this perfect symmetry: need. And then we started inventing new needs.

And then there was an excess and the system broke down. And now we have luxury products and desire. Since everything is broken, whatever desire is, it's logically prior, not necessarily chronologically, but logically prior. Consumerism didn't invent it. So one task we have is to disentangle desire from the way it's been captured by neoliberalism. And that includes of course the inverse of obesity, which is the middle-class desire to look thin and muscular and blissfully free, by virtue of the security of income, of the need for fat storage.

I had a very interesting experience: I was having breakfast, and these other people near me were having maybe one piece of toast, which wasn't even on the menu, without any jelly. It turns out they were from New York City, and were pointing at my breakfast and explaining it to these Australian guys, going, "That is typically Texan!" And I was like, "Actually this is just like scrambled eggs and hash browns. This is pretty much default." I didn't actually say anything, but I felt I was being made into a metonym for stupid, fat, working class, Southern people. It was this East Coast-y animus, which takes its pleasure in denial. As we subscend the neoliberal totality, we'll still find ourselves wanting things. "Want" is a good word, because it means "physically lack" and "crave." So we need to also make friends with craving and figure out ways not to cause people to suffer. Because craving and suffering helped propel us into this mess.

Back to Neanderthals liking Coke Zero, we were reading about the Haitian Revolution in my seminar last week and it was an excellent reminder as to what extent "globalization" as we know it today was driven in the first instance by desire for sugar, which in turn drove transatlantic slavery to secure plantation labor. I agree with you that we need to recognize the material basis of pleasure and craving, the chemicals and neurotransmitters that are involved in the operation of desire in a general sense. Neanderthals probably would have been quite happy to discover Coke Zero, they certainly would have loved the sugar that became an obsession to the Early Modern Europeans who got their tastebuds on it.

A sugar high was apparently so potent that it was worth organizing a global apparatus of agriculture, slave labor and transportation to make it available on demand. And through the Haitian Revolution's rejection of that apparatus, as Susan Buck-Morss teaches us, something like sugar actually came to impact political philosophy, indirectly, mediated a couple times over by folks like Hegel. But I also want to make the case for a feminist lens that as you say recognizes the subscendent multiplicity that is desire and avoids the transcendental definitional impulse to grasp Desire as a universal condition. I see that impulse even in more decentered and leaky theories of desire and pleasure like Foucault's through the focus on how relays of power constitute universalizing norms and institutions. Foucault is on the right path but it's still a discussion of desire that seems rather androcentric and of course Eurocentric in its coordinates. This is also, forgive me, one of my pet peeves about the call toward the posthuman. I keep hearing in it the boy-horror fantasy, "OK, the world is in terrible shape, and us boys seem incapable of controlling it anymore, so let's please get our extinction event over already and transcend off into some after-world." It feels like yet another act of narcissistic abandonment sometimes.

I don't think humans should allow themselves a posthuman condition. We can be transhuman, I'm all for that, or subhuman maybe. What I prefer about the hyposubject is that it seems to me to resist the endgame of blissful extinction that also happens to relieve us of all the responsibility. So maybe there actually is some value in having a couple of white guys sitting around and trying to come to terms with the fact that people like us have a particular responsibility for our present condition. Not to take a savior position but to try to commit ourselves to a program of rebecoming as something less dangerous. To reprogram.

I have this fear that if we white guys can't reprogram ourselves— the first act of which is simply to listen to what non-white non-guys have been telling us for a long time—then it's going to be very difficult to shift the trajectory of the Anthropocene. At least given the timeframes that science is telling us. But maybe those timeframes are also designed to stimulate heroic interventions by engineers and entrepreneurs, new legions of green hypersubjects. Repetition looming. I can't agree with you more. Although I would probably call "transhuman" that which you called "posthuman." It's just a terminological question. I did this radio interview about the singularity, and so I watched a lot of Ray Kurzweil's stuff.

And Ray Kurzweil is saying, death we are told is real, and we have to accept it. But I don't accept it, so freeze me, because won't it be good for the future when they open up my cryogenic tube and I, Ray Kurzweil, pop right out of it, and proceed to upload myself into the cloud. That's the desire loop right there and it's a boy fantasy, and the singularity as a metaphor involves being sucked into a totally black hole, dot dot dot. I mean come on now. The woman's body is again totally implicit in the fantasy: it's just a hole, a black hole. It's a perfect image, the fantasy of a wonderful, scary absence, which is sitting phobically on top of a much more threatening (to patriarchy) presence of actually existing beings – not just women, but all kinds of capital. Funnily enough, chattel, cattle, capital are all the same word. All these are the things that I would have at my disposal as a member of patriarchal agrilogistical space. But that arrangement is also insecure so it needs to be pinned together by desire. I was talking to a historian recently and I said, "Well, desire is logically prior to need." And he snapped back immediately with a default response, which he expressed thus: "We need salt." And I thought—I didn't say this, because I don't like arguing, especially at dinner—but first of all, these chips are exhibit A. They are the delivery mechanism for salt, sugar, fat. You have an off-switch in your brain for sugar interestingly.

You don't have an off-switch for salt. That means that you can't need salt, because there's never enough of it. And when you break it down to a single cell level, there's an ion channel exchanging chemicals and information between the cell wall and everything around it, and that involves sodium and potassium. Sometimes there's more sodium, which means the channel flows in manner x, and sometimes there's less sodium, which means it flows in manner y. But from moment to moment, there's no need for sodium. It's just that varying amounts of sodium across that barrier end up causing or inhibiting the flow of ions through the channel. So is that needing sodium? Do I need this building that I'm in right now? I'm in this building, and retroactively it's sheltering me from the sun, and has all these other properties. But I just stumbled into it somehow. This idea that you need something like salt or shelter also contains fear of death. You need because you don't want to die. If ecological awareness is anything, it's like Jae Rhim Lee in her mushroom death suit. It's exposing people to the fact that death is real and that the attempt to avoid it has precisely been Freud's death drive and/or Mary Daly's death culture. It's a necropolitics. Precisely, trying to avoid death, it is death. You can be death, or you can try to avoid death.

And this gets us back to the obesity question and what's distinctive about this era. What is distinctive about the contemporary economy of pleasure is that it's objective is apparently to stay in a pleasured state constantly, to stay as consistently high as possible, whether that's through sugar or alcohol or a variety of pharmaceuticals. We're talking about all my favorite hobbies!

I know, mine too. And exercise and fitness can participate in the same economy to the extent that one is chasing endorphin rushes there as well and you can even attach pleasure to pain. What has changed is that there's no longer oscillation, or, rather when one comes down, you're falling farther and faster than ever before. So that is medicalized too, as "depression," the retreat from pleasure, a pathological inability to get high on something despite the happy abundance of options. I find this striking in comparison to the part of Mexico where

I have been doing research, which is part of the global neoliberal apparatus but in a somewhat less fully realized way. This was a place where absence and inactivity were much more typical, time had a different character to it. Every moment did not exist as a vessel to recoup pleasure from. Other anthropologists have studied this dynamic. Marshall Sahlins once wrote an article called "The Original Affluent Society" about the organization of labor and luxury in the pre-modern world. And his thesis was basically that people worked intensively in short bursts to generate surpluses and then didn't do very much for several days. That was a more typical life rhythm before the industrial revolution. E.P. Thompson made a similar observation that one of the hardest challenges in creating a modern disciplined working class was getting people to show up for work at the same time every morning and to do roughly the same amount of work every day.

That required synchronized clocks and calendars, Ben Anderson's "empty linear time" and of course threats, violence and dispossession. But here's an interesting idea. What if an unexpected byproduct of that modern temporality was that now that we are working all the time, we expect the potentiation of pleasure at all times as well. We're never "off" so to speak. The brutality of factory labor conditions masked (and masks) that to a great extent. Those conditions seem toxic to pleasure. But flash forward ahead into the postfactory conditions that are enjoyed in many parts of the Global North and we are still working 24/7 but increasingly not under the sign of need but of convenience or even fun. Not that the jobs themselves are always pleasant—indeed a lot of them are what Graeber calls bullshit jobs— but they service a pleasure economy. So it's kind of appropriate to come to work stoned. We concentrate on getting and staying persistently high, maybe on food, maybe on drugs, maybe on sex, maybe on work itself. May I adumbrate? Yes, please.

I heard a lecture about beaches. It was by a Brazilian landscape designer who said, "If the beach is beneath the street, how do we make the street into the beach?" Let's look at Copacabana. Beaches are very interesting, because, precisely as you say, there can be experiences of laziness and boredom there, and given how difficult those experiences are to achieve, we like to fantasize about going to the beach. A cheap holiday in someone else's misery, as they say. So, to get metaphorical about it, let's find a way to have a cheap holiday in our own misery. That would be a subscendent strategy.

I think we agree that a big part of the issue with the Anthropocene is how to deal with certain magnitudes of energy use. Consumerism is obviously part of that problem, with all those flights to Caribbean beaches, but we continue to struggle to find the pressure points where that whole could be unmade. Subscendence helps by already revealing that consumerism is filled with vacancies and those vacancies point toward a practice of squatting, encouraging very small and seemingly insignificant occupations ubiquitously that can blindly participate in a more-ness that reforms our present conditions and relations in hopefully a less catastrophogenic direction.

Nonviolent or less violent – I think that's the key, rather than sustainable or resilient. People are talking about resilience. I'm not happy with either of those words. They're funny terms. Nonviolent, but let's cut to the chase, we need fewer life forms like ourselves. Tangentially, I read this piece in *The New York Times*: there's so much less rape and violence when there's a little bit of lithium in the water supply. This is now confirmed across Japan, Australia, America, and so some psychiatrists are thinking everybody needs a little bit, subclinical dose. But lithium is stigmatized, why? Well the author argued that it was because some dude died from a lithium treatment back in the 1940s.

And, obviously bipolar is stigmatized far more than depression, and lithium is the thing for that. But I think maybe it goes beyond that. Lithium is an atom. We don't make it. SSRIs, meanwhile, we think, oh SSRIs are complicated, made by expert people and carefully tested in a lab vs. this lithium that is just made by the sun. Interestingly just as Coca-Cola once had cocaine in it, 7-Up used to have lithium citrate in it. It was described as "lithiated lemon soda" until the 1940s. I didn't know that.

I didn't know that either. Lithium is very calming and it increases brain productivity and actually repairs some brain damage they're finding. So 7 Up wasn't Coke, right? It involved this metal, not even an organic chemical, but a metal from really low down on the table of elements. A simple crystal from the sun, you know. Why am I talking about this? It has to do with different modes of pleasure. But also nonviolence and the question of how one sparks a nonviolent transition.

Think about the opening of *The Thin Red Line* and the vision of paradise space as the opposite of war, or Gauguin and the Tahitians. The knee-jerk response—also evident in the Obeyesekere-Sahlins debate about what happened to Captain Cook in Hawaii—is, oh that's just primitivist; you're just making these people play a role in our drama. But what if that was also a ruse, in part, to keep the system going? The idea that modern life can't actually turn back because there's no reverse gear may be papering over the fact that the beach is beneath the street. It's already the case. We are just Tahitians titrating ourselves into this ridiculous clock-time. I saw this in Tibet. I saw mentally healthy, very poor people who needed money and clothes and food but not therapy sessions. And I puzzled, why? Well part of it is that consumer desire-time—if we're going to put it that way—isn't enough pleasure. Enough pleasure, because it kind of cuts you at the root. In five second's time we will now cease to enjoy ourselves this way and you have to go to a meeting. 4, 3, 2, now you have to be in this other mode.

There's no downtime. There's no follow-through. There's no recovery. Although so many of us do yoga, we can't talk about prana. We can't say, oh my chakras are all knotted up today, and I need some time to unknot them. You can't say, well, if we're going to get beyond the Cartesian dualism, we might have to find this third thing. Because we have the law of excluded middle, based on the law of non-contradiction, and we've all bought into that. Desire is thus very binaristic, there's mind and there's matter; there's subject, which is always human and usually white and male, and then there's the rest of the universe, which is an opaque black hole. There's no chance to allow things to be intermediate. The political challenge is trying to create spaces of intermediacy. We're living in a culture of either immediacy or infinite postponement of gratification. The desire loop has to do with infinite desire and therefore infinite dissatisfaction and infinitesimal immediate gratification simultaneously. I'm going to reach for the Coke, not because I'm a Neanderthal, but because I want to stave off the structurally coupled thought that my desire is infinite, which is making me crazy. But I should want everything. Does this make sense?

It does and speaking of mind, if it's not too tangential, I'd like to circle back to what happens after this lovely conversation and how I'll go off and write rejection letters for a journal I edit and who knows what you'll be on to next... I'd like to contextualize this in terms of the transformation of labor in the course of the 20th century. First there was the rise of Fordism and Taylorism and the domestication of a certain kind of machinic manual labor, working the lathe et cetera, and the normalization of assembly line factory production, and the logarithmic productivity that released.

But then it quickly became obvious—especially to those of us who grew up in urban areas in the 1970s with bad air, factory plumes and asthma everywhere—that that productive model compromised life and environment at every turn. So the pressure mounted to off-shore that labor—anti-union forces and environmental forces being temporarily in league on this point—and to send industry elsewhere, increasingly to Asia, so we could enjoy the fruits of industrial productivity but not suffer negative environmental effects. But then a dilemma arose: what are good middle class subjects in the Global North going to do with themselves if they're not working a factory job? We're still locked into a monetary economy that requires some kind of wage labor for survival. And that dilemma helped stimulate the evolution of a "knowledge economy" as part of the post-industrial order. I've been interested in mental labor for a long time as a socio-logical and anthropological phenomenon, and also in the post 1970s rise of the "intellectual." Not the high-thinker necessarily, just the person who thinks and manipulates knowledge for a living.

And so when I think about the two of us, I predict we're going to be doing a lot of thinking today. Many of our tasks will be loosely defined and rather open-ended in terms of their institutional commit-ments. But there is also no sense in which the workday of the mental laborer ever really ends; we will keep thinking until we sleep if we allow ourselves sleep. I don't want to overgeneralize our experience, because it is specific, but I think this is another aspect of the end of non-work. It's also an interface difference. In machinic manual labor, the interface is your lathe machine and you've got to turn the crank a certain number of hours a day. But you can't bring that mass of metal home with you from the factory. However, when you and I decide we want to do some "knowledge work," our tools and materials are in our memory, in our discourse and, nowadays, everywhere in the cloud. There's no home away from work which undoubtedly contributes to the stress of the mental laborer and the sense of needing to be con-stantly amped up to manage everything.

I'm having an extra thought about this which is perfectly apropos, because it has to do with this concept, dispositif and discourse of lei-sure. "Leisure time" meaning that people died so that we could have Sundays off and children didn't have to go up chimneys. In Marx and Engels there's an unbelievable categorization showing how capital-ists broke down the exact number of cubic inches that a human being could breathe in order to make their houses just that size. And give them exactly this many calories per day...With fewer people work-ing now, it truly reveals how capitalism is about exploitation of sur-plus labor time. Even leisure time is turning into labor now, especially with the Internet. The Internet started off in academia and the mili-tary and now it's everybody.

And what are they doing when they're posting on Facebook? Everybody is working to publicize themselves all the time; it's pre-cisely intellectual labor of the most annoying kind, a kind of bureau-cratic pencil-pushing of posting and commenting. But now everyone's doing it, so you have to sacrifice your entire Sunday to this intellec-tual labor. There's a war on free time that we're actively participating in. But it's deeply pleasurable somehow to eliminate our free time. For example, if you're on the beach and your best friend is fishing and not online, you're wondering: where the fuck are they? I want them; I'm lonely; I can't talk to them. I can't even know exactly how long they will be gone. I'm just gonna chill. There's nothing else to do; I'm gonna chill. I'm gonna wait, chill, chill-wait-anxiety. But friendly anxiety. This happened to me over the weekend. I'm writing an essay, and I'm Skyping with my co-writer, and I have to go to another meeting.

Boom! Lunch break. Then all of a sudden: where's my co-writer? And I've got all of these ideas and need help! All those emotions emerge from this standardization of leisure time and also the compulsion to fill it. There's a brilliant XTC song called "Leisure," which is about a guy who's been made unemployed, because his factory has been upgraded to robots. This is 1982 and "I'm drowning in leisure" is the chorus. You know, they teach me how to work, but they can't teach me how to shirk. We don't know how to shirk. Or how to just sit. Or how to wait as an art of being.

The model analogy in a way would be a carrion animal. I once described myself in an interview as a "spokes-vulture" for ecological awareness. We were talking about death and being eaten by vultures. And then about that kids movie where the vultures are the chorus and sit around commenting on all the main activity. And it's apropos because, anthropologically, we are carrion animals, aren't we? I mean, we don't just hunt game. Humans are scavengers as much as anything.

Scavengers and beachcombers. And thus the analogy to a vulture or some kind of carrion animal constantly waiting for their opportunity. But this identification is resisted. In the way in which loitering groups of young people are always seen as suspicious. They are criminalized even. More than three young people in New York—especially post-9/11—can be hauled off by the cops if they're just hanging around in social space. So if unplugging from the grid is about changing the energy throughput, when there's no gasoline to take me to the mall, I might have to walk there or cycle there or else I'm stuck here. I can't fulfill my desire to act like a predator, hunting up new experiences, so instead I have to accept my vulture status. Embrace your inner scavenger! It reminds me of that Joaquin Phoenix movie, *Her*. Oh, that. It's genius.

One of the things we immediately noticed was that everyone is wearing flannel pants in the future. And moving at a much slower pace. There is going to be a lot of sitting around outside apparently. That retemporalization was interesting as fantasy even if it was certainly depicted ambivalently. There was a grey sad purposelessness to all that slow time. Even though it was also depicted as a bit of victory to have put the default civilizational accelerationism behind us.

Part of the fantasy was that our new interactive digital technologies and artificial intelligence have finally provided us with our long-promised absolute leisure conditions. But of course we then discover that that leisure is empty and purposeless and filled with yearning. The message being that it's fine that what our actually-existing digital technologies did over the past thirty years was to recolonize our leisure time as forms of usually unwaged work. Patriarchy plus washing machines. Now there's so much more washing. Including washing your Facebook and Twitter and Tumblr accounts, to keep them shiny looking and fresh smelling.

There's so much maintenance. As Marx says, we've become an appendage of flesh on a machine of iron. Maintaining machineries is what we're about. Maybe not machines of iron but of silicon and electricity. Not to mention maintaining a smoothly functioning agrilogistical project. At all costs, we have to keep the smooth functioning going, and we have to keep the smooth functioning of smooth functioning going. We want to believe that every bit of sand can be made a pearl.

Is it time to go? Yes. But this will go on, no? Definitely. It's not up to us after all.

0.0002: some suggested readings & viewings

Sara Ahmed, *Living a Feminist Life*

Susan Buck-Morss, "Hegel and Haiti"

Ta-Nehisi Coates, "The First White President"

Alfonso Cuarón, *Gravity*

Gilles Deleuze and Félix Guattari, *A Thousand Plateaus*

Jacques Derrida, "There is No 'One' Narcissism"

Nick Estes, *Our History is the Future*

Denise Ferreira da Silva, *Toward a Global Idea of Race*

Shulamith Firestone, *Dialectic of Sex*

Sigmund Freud, *The Interpretation of Dreams*

Ganzeer, *The Solar Grid*

Jón Gnarr, *Gnarr!*

David Graeber, *Bullshit Jobs*

Donna Haraway, *The Companion Species Manifesto*

Graham Harman, *Object-Oriented Ontology*

GWF Hegel, *Phenomenology of Spirit*

Douglas Holmes, *Integral Europe*

Andrew Hussie, *Homestuck*

Luce Irigaray, *This Sex Which is Not One*

Hajime Isayama, *Attack on Titan*

NK Jemisin, *How Long 'til Black Future Month?*

Eduardo Kohn, *How Forests Think*

Karl Marx, *Grundrisse*

Marshall McLuhan, *Understanding Media*

Reza Negarestani, *Cyclonopedia*

Elizabeth Povinelli, *Geontologies*

Marshall Sahlins, "The Original Affluent Society"

Audra Simpson, *Mohawk Interruptus*

David Smith, *If*

Boots Riley, *Sorry to Bother You*

Hermann Scheer, *The Solar Economy*

Anna Tsing, *The Mushroom at the End of the World*

Raoul Vaneigem, *The Revolution of Everyday Life*

Denis Villeneuve, *Arrival*

Raymond Williams, *Marxism and Literature*

Jeff Vandermeer, *Borne*

Kathryn Yusoff, *A Billion Black Anthropocenes or None*

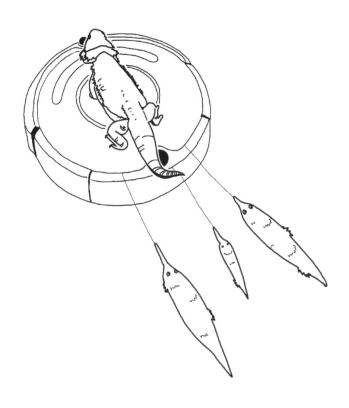

Lightning Source UK Ltd.
Milton Keynes UK
UKHW010636210721
387524UK00001B/104